CATHOLICISM – HINDUISM

Vedàntic Investigation of Raimundo Panikkar's Attempt at Bridge Building

Kana Mitra

UNIVERSITY
PRESS OF
AMERICA

LANHAM • NEW YORK • LONDON

BR
128
.H5
M57
1987

Copyright © 1987 by

University Press of America,® Inc.

4720 Boston Way
Lanham, MD 20706

3 Henrietta Street
London WC2E 8LU England

All rights reserved

Printed in the United States of America

British Cataloging in Publication Information Available

Library of Congress Cataloging-in-Publication Data

Mitra, Kana, 1936-
    Catholicism—Hinduism : vedantic investigation of
Raimundo Panikkar's attempt at bridge building.

    Bibliography: p.
    1. Christianity and other religions—Hinduism.
2. Catholic Church—Relations—Hinduism. 3. Hinduism—
Relations—Christianity. 4. Panikkar, Raimundo,
1918-   . 5. Catholic Church—Doctrines—History—
20th century. 6. Hinduism—Doctrines. I. Title.
BR128.H5M57 1987   261.2'45   87-2109
ISBN 0-8191-6157-8 (alk. paper)
ISBN 0-8191-6158-6 (pbk. : alk. paper)

All University Press of America books are produced on acid-free
paper which exceeds the minimum standards set by the National
Historical Publication and Records Commission.

CONTENTS

Preface: A Way to the Bridge

Raimundo Panikkar is a Catholic Christian? Raimundo Panikkar is a Hindu? He is both! How can one person believe that
Jesus Christ is the sole self-revelation in human form of the
one true God, and at the same time believe in the self-revelation
of the many gods of Hinduism? Of course one person cannot do
both, and Panikkar does not say he does. Rather, he argues that
both sides of this equation are distortions which have tended
to become fixed in many minds in unreflective fashion. He then
sets about trying to probe beneath the surfaces of each tradition
to search for a deeper, more authentic understanding--but with
a difference.

The difference is that Panikkar searches for the authentic
core of Christianity and of Hinduism not from the outside, but
from within, and from within both at the same time. There have
been many Christians who have studied Hinduism very deeply and
even sympathetically, but in the end they have remained Hindus
who have studied, and perhaps even absorbed elements of, Christianity. But Raimundo Panikkar is a believer in and follower of
both Hinduism and Christianity. If religion is understood as
"an explanation of the meaning of life and how to live accordingly," then Panikkar is one who has probed to the authentic
core of each tradition and lived accordingly.

But there is more, and that is what this book is about.
Raimundo Panikkar has not only learned and lived Hinduism and
Christianity, but he has also spent his life building a bridge
from core to core. He has--if I may be allowed to be a bit pun-
ny--"cor ad cor loquitur" (he "speaks heart to heart"). Those
Christians who search the works and life of Raimundo Panikkar
find an authentic Christian and true Christianity; those Hindus
who search the works and life of Raimundo Panikkar find authentic
Hinduism and a true Hindu. Both also find a bridge of learning
and living built between the two, and an invitation to walk that
bridge.

Kana Mitra has walked that bridge from the Hindu side.
Here, she provides a guide to all--Hindu, Christian, and
neither--to embark upon that exciting bridge journey. Come!

Leonard Swidler

iii

Introduction

A bridge between Catholicism and Hinduism
may seem to be impossible and hence absurd.
Catholicism is exclusivistic in its confession of
faith; Hinduism is usually considered as
inclusivistic. Catholicism and the different
traditions of Hinduism have different doctrines
about God or ultimate reality, humans, the world,
and the interrelationship between them. Perhaps
some similarities can be indicated along with
their differences as most of the scholars of
comparative religions do. Although a bridge does
not presuppose obliteration of all differences
rather--it presupposes the differences--yet in
order to have a bridge, some common foundations
must be found. Raimundo Panikkar as well as some
other contemporary Catholics believe that there
is a common ground between Catholicism and
Hinduism. They are engaged in dialogue with
Hinduism. For Panikkar dialogue with Hinduism is
the bridge or communication and even communion
between Catholicism and Hinduism.

The contemporary Catholics who are in
dialogue with Hinduism have complex reasons for
their endeavors. First, the Catholic confession
of faith makes dialogue a necessity. Second, the
historical situation of the contemporary world
makes dialogue inevitable and unavoidable in two
different ways: the global context of contemporary humans makes parochialism an impossibility;
the physical closeness of Catholics and Hindus
leads to mutual appreciation. Catholics are
impressed by the ennobling aspects of Hinduism.
Third, the non-Western Christians are troubled by
a sense of double identity, Christian and the
culture in which they are born. The need for a
bridge is a personal need for them. We shall try
to elaborate each of these points.

First, the Catholic confession of
faith makes dialogue with other religions a
necessity. Catholicism is exclusivistic in its
confession. The extreme expression of this
exclusivism was the statement of Pope Boniface
VIII in 1301.

We are required by faith to believe and hold
that there is only one Holy, Catholic and
Apostolic Church. We firmly believe it and
unreservedly profess it; outside it there is

v

neither salvation nor remission of sins....
Further, we declare, say, define and proclaim
that to submit to the Roman Pontiff is, for
every human, an utter necessity of Salvation.[1]

However, together with its exclusivity Catholicism at the same time believes in the universality of God's grace. Since the Fourth Lateran
Council, "extra ecclesian nulla salus" became an
explicitly stated doctrine of the Catholic
Church, but at the same time the Church accepted
the Scholastic dictum: "facienti quod est in se
Deus non denegat gratiam." Thus the defacto
existence of the plurality of religion is a very
difficult question for Catholicism. The
true-false schema of the relationship between
Catholicism and other religions of the world is
not acceptable as the common origin of humanity
is recognized as well as God's universal and
all-pervading grace. Prior to the conclusion of
the First Vatican Council in its <u>Schema
Constitutionis</u> <u>Dogmaticae</u> (1870), as well as in a
later period, in Pope Pius XII's encyclical
<u>Mystical</u> <u>Corpus</u> <u>Christi</u> (1948), a somewhat
liberal interpretation of Catholic exclusivism
was offered to accommodate plurality. Outside
the Church there is no salvation is interpreted
as without the Church there is no salvation,
i.e., those who are saved are saved by the Church
though they may not outwardly belong to the
institutional Church.[2]

However, this did not make room for other
traditions as such. The interpretation of
inclusivism and exclusivism continued. In the
Second Vatican Council it was declared for the
first time that not only Judaism but other
traditions also "reflect the ray of that truth
which enlightens all men."[3] The Second Vatican's
main concern was relationship with Judaism.
However, the other traditions also were included
in the end, although not much space was spent on
them in the documents of the Council. Some
Catholic theologians of the present day are
entering into dialogue with the different world
traditions in line with the declarations of the
Vatican II. They are trying to explore the
truths of other religions and attempting a more
inclusivistic interpretation of Catholic
exclusivism. Panikkar is one of the outstanding
figures among them.

Second, the contemporary historical situation of the world makes dialogue inevitable and unavoidable: a) The twentieth-century world is really physically one unit. Anything happening in one corner of the world can have a global impact. Parochialism is now anachronistic. One can no longer feel the security of living in one's own belief system or in one's own community; isolationism is almost a physical impossibility. The twentieth century is even transcending the global limit; its context is becoming interplanetary! Panikkar says that "any problem today which is not put in a universal context is, at least methodologically, wrongly posed."[4] Therefore, the ecumenism of the contemporary world is not an accident but a concession to the needs of time. Although ecumenism is quite popular yet there is skepticism and negativism about it. Sometimes it is considered the Esperanto of religion. It is seen to be generating a spirit of syncretism and also a kind of tolerance which is but another name for indifferentism. However, ecumenism, although it has pitfalls, does not attempt a sort of Esperanto of religion, as did the great Moghul King Akbar (1542-1605) in his Din-ilahi religion. It encourages an openness and dialogue which does not attempt to obliterate the distinctions between the different traditions, but develops both mutual and self-understanding by the traditions which are in dialogue. Pannikar's attempt at bridge building between Catholicism and Hinduism is a product of such ecumenism, which he himself names ecumenical-ecumenism, and Hillman elaborates in his book The Wider Ecumenism.

    b) The physical closeness with the Hindus are leading to the appreciation of Hinduism by the Catholics and they are moved towards a dialogue with them. In the different parts of the world Catholics are coming into everyday contact with Hindus. They know each other better. With familiarity the sense of cultural peculiarity and strangeness are weakening somewhat. Some nineteenth and twentieth century Hindu leaders and thinkers have made an impact on the Christian world. For example, many Christians admire Gandhi, Ramakrishna, Radhakrishnan; Henri Le Saux comes in close contact with the Hindu saint Raman Maharshi; Klaus

Klostermaier meets the bhakta in Vrindavan. They
can no longer maintain the attitude of the early
encounter period at which time the strangeness of
the Hindu practices often led the missionaries to
think that Hinduism was a false religion. They
are now attracted by the contemplative and the
meditative qualities of Hinduism. Bede
Griffiths, Henri Le Saux and Jules Monchanin try
to lead the life of Hindu sanyasi; they establish
Christian Ashramas. Henri Le Saux adopted the
name of Abhisiktananda, following the examples of
the Hindu monks. Abbé Monchanin assumed the new
name of Parama-Arubi-Anandam -"Supreme Formless
Bliss" which shows Hindu influence as well as his
adherence to the Holy Spirit.

Third, the need for dialogue with other
religions for many Catholics is a personal need.
This is typically exemplified in Panikkar.
Raimundo Panikkar's personal life is a bridge
between Hinduism and Catholicism. He was born of
an Indian Hindu father and a Spanish Catholic
mother. By nationality he is Indian, in
profession of faith he is Catholic--which
proclaims itself to be trans-national. His
scholarship in the tradition of his faith is well
recognized even if some of his interpretations
may be controversial. He is also well-versed in
Indian traditions--Hinduism and Buddhism--
particularly Hinduism, although his view of these
traditions is colored by his Christian stance.
He is not only intellectually familiar with both
sides of his heritage, he keeps in constant
physical contact with both of them. He studied
and taught in both the East and West. He
commutes between India and the United States.[5]
His very life is a dialogue between Catholicism
and Hinduism. The dialogue between the two is
not only his Catholic concern, it is also his
personal concern. In his writings there are
often hints to this effect. In The Unknown
Christ of Hinduism he mentions that the encounter
of religions takes place in the concrete reality
of our lives. "The encounter is the shock
produced by two realities"[6] in one heart. The
two traditions--Catholicism and Hinduism--may
agree and disagree on many points, "but the
historical, concrete and almost juridical fact
remains that on the one side stands Hinduism and
on the other Christianity. The born Indian
stands and is caught between."[7]

Panikkar represents the dilemma of all Indian-born Christians. This is the dilemma of all non-Western Christians. The issue of culture and religion is one of the important issues of Christian theology. The "Rethinking Christianity" group[8] of India are deeply involved with this issue. This brings out, and complicates, the need and importance of dialogue between Christians and non-Christian religions from the Christian perspective. If the Christians want to maintain their Christian identity as well as their cultural identity, a bridge has to be built between Christianity and the religious traditions of the non-Western cultures. Christianity needs to be interpreted in a more inclusivistic way and not be identified with its Western cultural form.

From the perspective of Hinduism the bridge building apparently does not seem to be important. Hinduism is considered an inclusivistic faith. The term Hinduism, which is geographical in its origin, is the common name for the many religious traditions of that geographical area. Traditional Hindus did not identify themselves as Hindus. A Hindu worships Visnu or Śiva or any other deity, may even worship Jesus Christ as his ideal deity and would usually identify himself/herself accordingly. However, used as a common name, the term Hinduism implies adherence to the supreme, universal and eternal Truth which appears in different ways in different traditions. In this sense, Christianity also would be considered a form of Hinduism. One can often encounter sectarianism in Hinduism. Śaivas and Vaisnavas may claim superiority over each other's tradition. Śaivas and Śāktas may be in conflict with each other. In the contemporary period, whereas the Vedāntin monks of the Rāmkrishna order preach many ways of salvation, Swāmi Bhakti-Vedānta of the Krishna Consciousness group proclaims the development of Krishna Consciousness as the only way to salvation. In Hindu religious groups, though anathemas were not pronounced on believers of other doctrines, in the Dharma Śāstras there are various prohibitions and restrictions about relationships with the mlechhas (those belonging to foreign faiths). However, the history of Hinduism in general indicates the peaceful coexistence of many faiths, and this reflects the spirit of the Rg-Vedic saying: "ekam sat vipra Vahudha vadanti" ("the truth is one, people speak of it in different ways"). This statement, though it advocates plurality, is considered in itself an exclusivistic statement. It is in direct opposition to the exclusivistic statement of Catholicism. The Hindus are proud of their tolerance. The attitude of the Hindus to other religions is typically expressed by Anandocoomar-swammy: "Our position in relation to the Christians and other faiths can be stated by saying that even if you are not on our side we are on yours, and this is something all your zeal cannot take away from us."[9] This may appear to be magnanimous, but it may not be less offensive than the doctrine of anonymous Christians. To pretend to know others and even to make room for others when the other does not understand you is considered arrogance by some. The Hindus, particularly some contemporary Hindu apologists who are called by Westerners as Neo-Hindus, seem to be as arrogant to the Christians as the exclusivistic claim of Catholicism seems arrogant to the Hindus. To be true to their spirit of tolerance, Hindus must take Catholics seriously and engage in dialogue with them.

Contemporary Catholics are interested in dialogue with Hinduism. This requires an attitude of openness which was not always present in the history of Catholicism. Catholicism, where it is not indifferent to other religions, can and actually has taken several attitudes toward them. The first is the attitude that non-Catholic religions are false religions. This can be traced back to the Gospels, where there is sufficient evidence of the condemnation of false religions. In his encounter with India, even a holy person like Francis Xavier said that all Hindus, especially the Brahmins, were "devil worshippers," the Buddhists "atheists," and Moslems "infidels."[10] The second attitude tries to draw an analogy between what Catholicism considers to be the relationship between Judaism and Christianity and the relationship between the non-Judaeo-Christian religions and Christianity. Christianity is the fulfillment of Judaism. In an analogical way it is also the fulfillment of other religions. Thus all other religions are subordinated to Christianity. This trend of thought was Protestant in origin. In the early twentieth century, J. N. Farquhar published The Crown of Hinduism, propagating this idea. Since then, volumes have been written in this spirit:

P. Devanandan's The Gospel and the Renascent Culture; W. Steward's Indian's Religious Frontiers: Christian Presence Amid Modern Hinduism; and Ishananda Vempeny's Inspiration In the Non-Christian Scriptures. This attitude can be contrasted to the attitude that Christianity is in radical discontinuity with the other religions. A radical presentation of this view is Hendrik Kraemer's The Christian Message In a Non-Christian World. However, the doctrine of fulfillment, in the end, believes in the ultimacy and supremacy of Christian revelation. Among the contemporary Catholic theologians in dialogue with Hinduism, R. C. Zaehner can be considered as an adherent of this view.

The third attitude which Panikkar, as well as Henri La Saux, describes as the attitude of Metanoia, is similar to the attitude of fulfillment in the sense that it also believes that Christianity is the fulfillment of each of the true religions. However, there is a fine shade of difference between this attitude and the fulfillment idea which enables it to be viable in the attempt at bridge building between Catholicism and other religions.[11] This attitude believes in conversion of all religions by Christ, but not in the Western form of Christianity. Further, conversion is understood in a special sense. It is not proselytization in the sense of making something different. It is a process of maturation from within, in the individual, as well as in the whole civilization. Therefore, Metanoia does not mean the conversion of the religions into Christianity in the sense of their all being absorbed in the grand totality of Christianity, but in their death and resurrection with Christ as that religion itself not as according to the fulfillment idea that religions become Christianity. Hinduism, in order to be fulfilled, has to die, but when it is resurrected, it is not a different religion--it is Hinduism. In the same way historical Christianity also has to go through the process of transformation. It is not yet perfect. It is also on the way. Another characteristic of this attitude which distinguishes it from the fulfillment idea, is that its view is not a one-way traffic from Christianity to other religions. Christianity as it is now in its historical form can also learn from and be enriched by the other traditions. This idea of

<u>Metanoia</u> is present in Jules Monchanin and Henri
Le Saux. Panikkar explicates its implications to
its fullest extent and with all its radicality,
as we shall see subsequently.

The Catholics of the twentieth century who
are engaged in a close encounter with Hinduism
and who believe in the continuity between
Hinduism and Christianity, can be classified
under two categories: the non-missionaries who
are primarily scholars, although committed to
Christianity, and the missionaries who, although
scholars, aim to evangelize. However, these
evangelists no longer believe in the attitude
which was expressed even in the earlier part of
this century in <u>Maximum Illud</u> of Pope Benedict
XV, who expressed the aim of missionary activity
as "to bring light to those dwelling in shadow of
death and to open the way to heaven to those
hurrying to destruction."[12]   Among the
non-missionary scholars, J. A. Cuttat, O. Lacombe
and R. C. Zaehner are well known. These scholars
are different in their attitudes from the earlier
Orientalists like Max Muller and Sylvain Levi,
who had more of a secular than religious
interest. They had an open mind on the
horizontal plane and did not care much about the
vertical. These later scholars in contrast, not
only want a horizontal openness, but vertical
depth as well. All three of these have been
consultants to the Roman <u>Secretariat for Non-
Christians</u>, whose secretary in 1980 is Cardinal
Pignedoli. Cuttat, Lacombe and Zaehner have only
had limited contact with India. Cuttat and
Lacombe lived in India in an official capacity as
ambassadors for short periods. Zaehner's
relationship was scholarly. Cuttat's knowledge
of Hinduism is limited, whereas Lacombe and
Zaehner are well known scholars of Hinduism. All
of them believe in the positive values of
Hinduism.

Cuttat's major principle of approach to
Hinduism is "contrast and convergence," as is
present in the pattern of the Hypostatic Union.
He does not propose to encounter Hinduism on the
doctrinal level, but on the level of spiritual
experience.[13] Although a committed Catholic,
Lacombe indicates how the spiritual élan of
Hinduism can enrich Christianity and the whole of
humanity. The thrust of his writings is on how
Hinduism can enrich Christianity.[14] He does not

xii

rule out doctrinal encounter, but believes that
one has to go to the elan to find the connection.
He is concerned about Hinduism's losing its
distinctive quality by being converted into
Christianity. In one of his articles he says,
"Let us ask God that India be for Christ. Let us
also pray that her entry into the visible church
be not after a cataclysm which would destroy the
deepest and the purest of her identity."[15]

R. C. Zaehner's approach actually belongs in
the fulfillment category. In his different works
he has tried to show how Hinduism evolved from
polytheism, to pantheism to monotheism, or
worship of a personal god, and, ultimately, how
all religions converge in Christ.[16] Consequently, his emphasis is on the bhakti tradition of
Hinduism and the importance of the Bhàgavad-Gità.

Among the missionaries, P. Johanns, Jules
Monchanin, Henri Le Saux, Klaus Klostermaier and
Dom Griffiths are very important. Some of them
were attracted by the philosophical systems of
Hinduism. Others by the monastic life. Johanns
had an intellectual, doctrinal perspective. In
the journal, Light of the East,[17] he developed
his major work: "To Christ Through Vedants." He
tried to show how Hinduism is the praeparatio
evangelica and found its fulfillment in Christ.
He mentioned the intention of the mission: "What
we...wish...to do is... to help India... to know
and understand Jesus.... We have no intention to
put out the existing lights. Rather, we shall
try to show that the best thought of the East is
a bud that fully expanded blossoms into Christian
thought."[18] Johanns lived in India for a long
time. He had to go back to Belgium because of
ill health, and died in 1955.

The other missionaries take a
contemplative-monastic approach, though many of
them do not disregard the doctrinal perspective.
Monchanin was a pioneer in adopting monastic life
in India following the Hindu tradition. He
considered India the Land of the Trinity.[19] His
mission was the conversion of India in its
totality to Christianity. He thought that it was
possible only by the practice of a monastic
contemplative life centered on the Holy Trinity,
which to him was the fulfillment of all the
aspirations of Hinduism. He came to India in
1939, and together with Dom Le Saux from France,

founded an Ashram dedicated to Trinity Saccidananda in South India, and called it
Shātivanan--The Wood of Peace. He wrote a few
books by himself and some with Henri Le Saux. In
all of them he stated that to meet Hinduism,
Christians have to go to its heart, i.e., the
mystical experience, and go through the process
of adoption, purification and transformation.
Christ assumed humanity so that humanity can
share in divinity. Following this model, a
missionary has to adopt the civilization to which
he is sent; he is to adopt and become the people
to whom he is sent, his people. Adoption is not
a simple trick, but is inherent in the principle
of charity underlying incarnation. Christ did
not simply pretend to be human, but became human.
Adoption should go hand in hand with purification. Sin has touched and distorted all
civilizations. Socio-cultural values have to be
purified from errors and distortions. The
missionary does not dictate the correction, but
himself goes through the suffering of his people.
He follows the example of death on the cross.
This is the second moment for salvation. This
leads to the third moment of salvation, i.e.,
transformation and glorification. This is the
total conversion and leads to the final
glorification at the parusia. Monchanin believes
that religion is the central part of all
civilization. Therefore, religion of the people
has to be adopted, purified and transformed.

What aspect of Hinduism has to be adopted,
Monchanin discussed in "L'Eglise et la Pensée
Indienne." He does not believe in indiscriminate
adoption of everything, but the adoption of the
true essence of Hinduism. He mentions the
difficulties of differentiating the kernel from
the husk. Hinduism developed through the
mixtures of Aryan and Dravidian civilizations.
The chronology of the Hindu scriptures are
difficult to determine. What is original and
what is superimposed is difficult to find. This
is true not only of Hinduism but of Christianity
also. However, he thinks that in the case of
Christianity, it is relatively easier as no summa
actually superceded the theology of Paul and
John. By his meditation and assimilation of the
Hindu scriptures he came to the realization that
in Hinduism there is a thirst for knowledge of
God and unity with God. This is the essential
life force of Hinduism. India is rich in this

xiv

respect. He thinks that in Greece there was only
'man-created mythology' which needed to be
converted by divine revelation. India's claim is
the possession of a revelation which emphasizes
the primacy of spirit and hence a search for the
Absolute beyond name and form.

Monchanin came to the conclusion that the
Trinity, particularly the Holy Spirit, the
"formless" person, would quench India's thirst
for "one without a second." He was convinced that
India was "awaiting the revelation of the mystery
of the Trinity, inaccessible equally to
metaphysical genius as well as to holiness."[20] He
said: It is in the inviolable sanctuary of a
meditating conscience that the encounter between
India and Christianity will take place."[21] He
lived the austere life of the Hindu sannyasi
while he was in India. However, his health
failed, and he returned to Paris and died there
in 1957.

Henri Le Saux followed the work of
Monchanin. He wrote extensively.[22] His works
Hindu-Christian Meeting Point and Saccidananda
show his adherence to Monchanin's view that the
meeting point between Hinduism and Christianity
is in what the Hindus call the "cave of the
heart." In his work Saccidananda he did not start
directly with the doctrinal comparison
of Vedànta and Christianity, but with the life
story of a Hindu saint, Ramana Maharshi. He
believes that a Christian who wants to be in
dialogue with Hinduism needs to have a special
kind of disposition. This is the inward
disposition, or what the schoolmen called
habitus, of recollection and contemplation. A
superficial acquaintance with the folklores of
India would not do. He needs to be acquainted
with the Indian traditions no doubt. Moreover he
needs some inner preparation himself.

He needs the "knowledge of those ultimate
depths of the self," the "cave of the heart,"
where the Mystery revealed itself to the
awareness of the rishis. It is only here, in
the secret place of the "welling up," of the
"source," as Raman Maharshi called it in his
Upadesa saram, that a true dialogue can
begin.[23]

In Hindu-Christian Meeting Point, he described
how some Christians were trying to go to the
inner depth of Hindu spirituality and relate it
to their Christian experience. Henri Le Saux, or
as he is better known, Abhisiktananda, comes to
the conclusion:

> The preparation into man's ontological depth
> which is realized in Vedantic experience,
> certainly seems to be the highest possible
> preparation of the human spirit for its entry
> into the depths of God and for discovering
> there the ultimate secret of its own being.[24]

Abhisiktānanda died in 1973.

Klaus Klostermaier is currently not
extensively involved in actual dialogue between
Hinduism and Christianity, but his important
works on Hindu-Christian dialogue[25] show that he
also is a believer in the dialogue in depth and
not simply in intellectual dialogue. For him
dialogue simply on intellectual level is
"armchair dialogue."

> In real dialogue Hindu and Christian partners
> very soon realize the relativity of their
> philosophies and theologies, the need to go
> beyond conceptual formulas, to find truth and
> reality. "Dialogue in depth" moves on the
> level of spirituality--only here can true
> "understanding" ever be achieved.[26]

This comes out very clearly in the Hindu and
Christian in Vrindavan. Although the content of
this book cannot be summarized here, it should be
noted that it is the description of the
experience of challenge and enrichment of the
author, a Christian, by the whole atmosphere of
Vrindavan. Klostermaier very clearly shows the
shallowness of mere intellectual dialogue or
dialogue on the doctrinal level. He thinks that
genuine dialogue is a challenge--a challenge of
truth which crushes everything under its wheel.

> Dialogue challenges both partners, takes them
> out of the security of their own prisons
> their philosophy and theology have built for
> them, confronts them with reality, with
> truth: a truth that cannot be carried home
> black on white, a truth that cannot be left

to gather dust in libraries, a truth that
demands all.[27]

In his personal encounter with Hindus and
Hinduism he could realize why Hindus do not find
anything new in Christianity. Christ in
Christianity is named the Son of God. In India
this idea has been present from time immemorial.
"Rāma Rājya" may be the political slogan of a
particular party, yet its significance is not
different from the kingdom of God. He says:

> The more I learnt of Hinduism, the more
> surprised I grew that our theology does not
> offer anything essentially new to the
> Hindu--that even some of the problems had
> been treated much more subtly and circumstan-
> tially by Hindu scholars than by our
> Christian ones. And yet--even if we should
> discover that the Gospels do not say anything
> "new" either in content or theologically, the
> "vocation" of the Christian would be as
> meaningful--absolutely new and original on
> the existential level--as God-experience. In
> many respects this experience is the exact
> opposite of Vedantic realization of Brahman.
> And this is the starting point: for the
> proclamation of Christ in India we do not
> need Greek philosophy nor Western science.
> We must render audible the "call" of Christ
> within the words and structures of Indian
> thought.[28]

According to Klostermaier Christ is the Truth.
Anyone who thinks that he has already deciphered
that truth never realizes it--only those who are
on the way finally arrive at it. John says that
Logos is prōstòn théòn. Christ is present where
there is "movement toward God." No other category
is adequate. In the concluding part of this book
Klostermaier writes:

> Christ is not an idea, Christ is not an
> emotion, Christ is not a religious museum--
> piece--Christ is the Logos of God; in the
> encounter with Hinduism I have begun to
> understand how Christ meets the Hindu--not
> from the outside, but within his own thought
> and faith.[29]

Dom Bede Griffiths still lives in India in
the Benedictine Ashrama and follows the life of

Sanyāsi. He is still very much involved in actual dialogue and contributes to different journals. He has written several books on the Hindu-Christian themes.[30] His view is similar to the ideal of dialogue in depth. He says:

> What I really hope for is that we realize the reality of this mystical experience, of the absolute in our lives. Then we may meet the Hindu in the heart of his religion, and in the heart of our religion. This is the meeting place, what Abhisiktananda called the Hindu-Christian meeting point in the cave of the heart. I think that we, as monks, as Benedictines all of us religious in India, have this particular vocation, to bring this experience into our lives, as far as we can as limited human beings, and to open ourselves to this experience and at the same time open ourselves to the Hindu at his deepest level of experience and help him to realize himself more fully.[31]

Griffiths believes in two-way traffic between Christianity and Hinduism. He relates how they can mutually enrich each other. However, in all his writings his approach is comparative rather than introductory of any new interpretation of either Hinduism or Christianity in the light of each other. He believes that only in the sphere of the intuition of the ultimate there is convergence.

> There is a final transcendent state of being and consciousness, in which alone perfect bliss is to be found, to which every great religion bears witness.[32]

Most of the contemporary Catholics in dialogue with Hinduism believe in dialogue in depth. They believe in some common ground between Hinduism and Christianity. Some have come up with proposals and programs of how a Christian should prepare for such an encounter; for example, Monchanin, Abhisiktānanda. Some make doctrinal comparisons between Hinduism and Christianity, for example, Griffiths. Of the Catholics, Griffiths is the only living person who is actively engaged in dialogue with Hinduism. However, so far his contribution has been limited to comparative studies only.

In Raimundo Panikkar we encounter dialogue
in depth, doctrinal comparison, and reinterpretation of Catholicism in the light of dialogue with
Hinduism. Thus in him we find representation of
all the Catholics who are in dialogue with
Hinduism. In him we encounter dialogue in the
special sense of the term, i.e., neither mere
comparison of the two traditions, nor debate or
monologue. He listens as well as speaks. He
tries to understand Hinduism from the perspective
of a Hindu, the best that a Catholic can, and he
tries to integrate that understanding into
Catholicism, the best that a committed Catholic
can. He is acquainted with the writings of the
Catholics who are in dialogue with Hinduism. He
is aware of the problems that a Catholic
encounters in his dialogue with Hinduism. He
wants to be true to the concerns of these
Catholics, to their Catholic commitments but at
the same time he is sensitive to the commitments
of the Hindu, his dialogue partner. He wants to
speak in a way as to be understood by him. In
the light of his dialogue with Hinduism he
attempts reinterpretation of Christianity.
Klostermaier is the only other Catholic who
reinterpreted Christian doctrines in the light of
dialogue with Hinduism. In <u>Kristavidya: A
Sketch of an Indian Christology</u>, he attempted to
present a Christology not in terms of Western
Christianity but in terms of Hindu spirituality.
However, this interpretation does not show any
link to the historical traditions of Christianity. Panikkar tries to be faithful to
historical traditions of Christianity and yet
interpret them to be understood by a Hindu. Thus
in him bridge building between Catholicism and
Hinduism had more potential than among any other
Catholic that is in dialogue with Hindu.
Panikkar's personal situation is a representation
of the schizophrenic situation of most of the
non-Western Christians. For him, as for most of
the non-Western Christians, bridge building is a
personal existential need. Therefore, his
attempt is not a complacent, comfortable,
armchair dialogue, but a vital and even daring
and radical one. In him we find Hindu-Christian
dialogue in all its radicality and potentiality.

    The rational behind the attempt at vedāntic
investigations of Panikkar are several. First,
it enables us to evaluate Panikkar according to
his own criterion. According to Panikkar,

dialogue can be considered as fruitful if the
partners of dialogue can understand if not accept
each other. Thus Vedàntic response is meaningful
to find out if Panikkar's view is acceptable from
their perspectives.

Secondly, from the Catholic perspective most
of the Catholics who are in dialogue with
Hinduism found in Vedànta a challenge, as well as
a possible enrichment for Christianity. Most of
them indicated that at the core of Hindu
spirituality lies the quest for oneness, for
non-duality. This to them, when not interpreted
as monism, is a pure form of spirituality that is
expressed in any non-Christian religion. For
example, Abhisiktànada said:

> The advaitic experience which is the heart of
> Hinduism is beyond question the highest point
> attainable by man in the contemplation of the
> mystery of man and nature.[33]

Griffiths indicated that the mystical experience
of the Absolute is the enrichment of spirituality. P. Johanns showed how one can arrive at
Christ through Vedànta.

Panikkar also thinks that Hindu spirituality
is essentially mystical and the urge toward unity
is its basic urge. However, he believes that
advaita specifically can help to lead to a deeper
understanding of the Trinity.[34] Many of the
Catholics following the Hindu-Catholic Brahmavandhav Upadhya believe that Vedànta can do the same
service for Christianity in India as Greek
philosophy did for Europe. Through Greek
philosophy Jewish Christianity made sense to
Gentile Europe. Similarly, Vedànta being the
essential element of the Hindu spirituality, it
would make Christianity intelligible to India.
Thus a Vedàntic response is significant for the
Catholics.

Thirdly, from the Hindu perspective Vedàntic
investigation of Panikkar is meaningful not
simply because most of the contemporary Hindu
thinkers have a Vedàntic world-view, but also
because some of them are engaged in a
counter-apologetic against Christianity.[35]
Although the Vedàntins--at least many contemporary advocates of it like Ràmakrishna and
Gandhi--maintain the equality of all religions,

it seems that they believe in the superiority of
Vedānta insofar as it can provide a basis for a
universal religion, rather than Christianity,
which tends to emphasize a particular event in
history. Some of the contemporary Vedāntins
worked out a Christology from the Vedāntic
perspective which poses a challenge as well as
some new possibilities to the traditional
Christological thinking of Christianity.
Panikkar is aware of these challenges and has
addressed himself to many of the problems that
have been raised by the Hindu thinkers. An
investigation of Panikkar from their perspective
would show the success or failure of Panikkar's
bridge-building. A Vedāntin can see whether and
how far Panikkar's inclusivistic exclusivism is
compatible with his exclusivistic inclusivism.

Fourthly, a Vedāntic investigation of
Panikkar would be interesting also from the
scholarly perspective as it would highlight the
problems as well as the possibilities of the
dialogue between two opposing truth claims. The
Catholic and the Vedāntic, especially the
advaitic, world views are apparently very
different. Is it possible to have any dialogue
between exponents of the two? Thus Panikkar's
attempt at bridge building between Catholicism
and Hinduism and a Vedāntic investigation of it,
in addition to showing the possibilities and the
problems of encounter between these two
traditions, would also reflect some light on the
problems of inter-religious dialogue in general.
In the face of absolute truth claims is it
possible to have religious dialogue? Does
dialogue ultimately amount to debate or at the
most to comparative religion? What are the
requirements of dialogue--what are its rules?
What does it aim for?

We shall present our discussion under two
parts. In the first part we shall start with
Panikkar's idea of what religious dialogue is,
its requirements, and its aims. Then, following
his own schema, which requires understanding the
partner in dialogue first and then integration of
it in one's own tradition, we shall present his
understanding of Hinduism and then his reflections on Christian doctrine in the light of his
understanding of Hinduism. We shall try to
investigate how far this is acceptable from the
perspective of Catholicism. The second part is a

Vedāntic investigation of Panikkar. So far no
written response has been made to Panikkar from
any Vedāntic perspective. Therefore, we shall
first present some Christological reflections of
some modern Hindu thinkers and relate them to
Panikkar's thinking. Then we shall compare the
world-views of two important schools of Vedānta,
Advaita and Viśistādvaita, and Panikkar's
world-view, and thereby investigate whether and
how far it is possible to respond positively to
Panikkar from their perspectives.

Notes

Introduction

[1] "Unam Sanctam," in J. Neuner and J. Dupis (eds.), The Christian Truth (Dublin: Mercier Press, 1973), pp. 210f.

[2] Peter Schreiner, "The Attitude of Catholic Theology Towards the Non-Christian Religions." (Thesis submitted in partial fulfillment for Masters of Art Degree, Temple University, Oct. 20, 1968), p. 16.

[3] Nostra Aetate, 2.

[4] Raimundo Panikkar, "The Relationship of Gospel to Hindu Religion and Culture," Jesus and Man's Hope. Pittsburgh: Pittsburgh Theological Seminars, 1970-1971. Vol. 11: p. 247.

[5] Some bibliographical reference to Panikkar is available in Journal of Ecumenical Studies, vol. 11 (Winter 1974): p. 109. Also Cross Current, vol. 29, nr. 2.

[6] Panikkar, The Unknown Christ of Hinduism (London: Darton, Longman, and Todd, 1964), p. 11.

[7] Ibid., p. 12.

[8] This is a group of Christian thinkers who are trying to Indianize Christianity. The source of this movement was the publication of the book Rethinking Christianity in India by J. V. Job and others from Madras in 1938. Chenchia, Devanandan and Thomas all belong to this group. In Bangalore the Institute of Religion and Society is involved in this task. The journal published by this institute is their mouthpiece.

[9] Cf. Orientalia, 1946, p. 33, quoted by Cyril B. Papali in "Excursus on Hinduism," Commentary on the Doctrines of Vatican II. Vol. III. N. Y.: Harder á Harder, 1969, p. 137.

[10] Griffiths, Christ in India. N. Y.: Charles Scribners and Sons, p. 58.

[11] E. Sharpe, Faith Meets Faith (London: S.C.M., 1977), p. 128. Sharpe thinks that Panikkar's view is not different from "fulfillment" idea of Farquhar. It may seem true in the light of early Panikkar. But 1982 new and revised edition of The Unknown Christ of Hinduism, Panikkar states that his idea of fulfillment is not the obliteration of the different tradition but each is fulfilled within its distinctiveness.

[12] Acta Apostolica Sedis. 11 (1919) 446. Quoted in J. Mattam, The Land of Trinity, p. 10.

[13] For Cuttat's view see, J. A. Cuttat, Expérience chrétienne et Spiritualité Orientale (Paris: Desclee, 1960).

[14] O. Lacombe, although he worked in official capacity in India, pursued primarily an academic career, and published an enormous amount of works. For his view about relationship of Hinduism and Christianity see his Chemin de l'Inde et Philosophie Chrétienne (Paris: Aloatia, 1956) and the article, "La Recontre des Religions," Nova et Vetera, 43 (1968), 2, pp. 104-118.

[15] Lacombe, "Elan Spirituel de l'Hinduisme," Bulletin du Cercle St. Jean Baptist, n. 24, (June-July, 1963), quoted in J. Mattam, Land of Trinity. Bangalore, India, (TPI, 1975), p. 45.

[16] R. C. Zaehner also has an enormous amount of publication. For his view of the relationship of Hinduism and Christianity, see The Convergent Spirit (London: Routledge and Kegan Paul, 1963), The Catholic Church and World Religions (London: Burnes and Oates, 1964), Concordant Discord (Oxford: 1970).

[17] Light of the East was an enterprising review started by some young missionaries of India, inspired by Brahmavandhav Upadhya, who asserted himself to be Hindu-Catholic. G. Dandoy and P. Johanns in collaboration with Animananda, a disciple of Brahmavandhava, started this work at Calcutta, India in 1922.

[18] The Light of East, 1 (1922): p. 1-2, quoted in Mattam, Land of Trinity, p. 20.

[19] Jules Monchanin, Ecrits Spirituels, Presentation d'Edourd Buperray, ed. du Centurion (Paris 1957), p. 37, quoted in Mattam, Land of Trinity, p. 144. Other works of Monchanin include: A Benedictine Ashram (coauthor Henri Le Saux), first published as An Indian Benedictine Ashram (Saccidananda Ashram, Tiruchirapalli, 1951; rev. ed., Douglas: Times Press, 1964); Ermites du Saccisananda: Un essai d,integration Chrétienne de la tradition monastique de l'Inde (with Le Saux), 2nd ed. (Casterman, 1957); Mystique de l'Inde, Mystére Chretienne (Fayard, 1974).

[20] Monchanin, "L'Inde et la Contemplation," Dieu Vivant, 1 (1945), p. 23, quoted in Mattam, The Land of Trinity. p. 157.

[21] Monchanin, Ecrits Spirituels, p. 127, quoted in Mattam, p. 157.

[22] Works by Henri Le Saux (Abhisiktananda), Hindu-Christian Meeting Point (ISPCK, 1976, first English ed., 1969); Saccidananda: A Christian Approach to Advaitic Experience (ISPCK, 1974); The Further Shore (ISPCK, 1975).

[23] Abhisiktananda, Hindu-Christian Meeting Point. Delhi, (ISPCK, 1969), p. 6.

[24] Abhisiktananda, Hindu-Christian Meeting Point (ISPCK, 1976), p.117.

[25] One important example is K. Klostermaier, In the Paradise of Krishna (Philadelphia: Westminster Press, 1971).

[26] Klostermaier, "Hindu-Christian Dialogue," Journal of Ecumenical Studies 5 (1968), pp. 33-34.

[27] Klostermaier, Hindu and Christian in Vrindavana. P. 103.

[28] Ibid., pp. 109, 117.

[29] Ibid. 117.

[30] Among the books are, Christ in India (New York: Charles Scribners and Sons, 1966) and Vedanta and Christian Faith (Los Angeles: Dawn Horse Press, 1973).

[31] Dom Bede Griffiths, "The Advaita Experience and the Personal God in the Upanishads and Bhagavad Gita," Indian Theological Studies, Patristics and Indian Spirituality, vol. 15, (March, 1978), no. 1, pp. 85-86.

[32] Dom Bede Griffiths, Vedanta and Christian Faith. p. 84.

[33] Griffiths, "The Advaita Experience and the Personal God in the Upanishads and Bhagavad Gita," pp. 85-86.

[34] Panikkar, The Trinity and Religious Experience of Man, N. Y.: Orbis Books, 1973.

[35] Vivekananda, Complete Works. 5 vols. Almora: Advaita, 1931, Ashrama, Introduction; D. S. Sharma, The Renaissant Hinduism. Bombay: Bharatiya Vidya Bhavan, 1966.

Part I

Panikkar's Dialogue with Hinduism

Chapter 1

Panikkar on Dialogue

Bridge-building between different religions,
according to Panikkar, is possible through
dialogue, or, rather, dialogue itself is the
communication and sometimes communion between
them. The term dialogue has been used by different scholars on religion in so many different
ways[1] and the requirements and aims of dialogue
also have been viewed in such diverse ways[2] that
it is necessary to have some clarity about what
Panikkar means by dialogue, what he thinks its
requirements are and its aim is. In this chapter
we shall attempt to indicate the meaning of
dialogue as it is presented by Panikkar to
determine its characteristics as distinguished
from debate and comparative religion with which
it is often confused. According to Panikkar
religious dialogue is essentially a religious act
and as such not subject to any hard and fast
formal rules. Yet, we shall try to develop some
criterion and guide lines from his own presentations in order to evaluate him by his own criterion.

Panikkar's views about the requisites for
and aims of dialogue have gone through some
modifications, as can be noted from his earlier
to his later writings. However, all along he has
considered dialogue between religions as itself
religious and hence a sacred act. In his earlier
writings, e.g., The Unknown Christ of Hinduism
(1964), he said:

The meeting of religions is not merely an
intellectual endeavor, not a simply practical
problem; it is in itself a religious experience and religious task; it is the meeting of
God in my friend who follows another path and
perhaps even denies God--or at least my
conception of God--for though I cannot help
having a conception of my own, the living God
I worship is not an ideal of my mind, a
concept, but transcends all understanding.
Religions meet where religions take their

1

source. Religions do not meet merely in
ideas or in ideals. Religions meet in
religion.[3]

For Panikkar, therefore, religious dialogue is
not comparative religion. It is not finding the
parallels and divergences of the different
religious traditions. Here the question is more
radical.

The integral question is not, for instance,
whether the idea of "grace" in Saivism is
similar to the idea of "grace" according to
Christianity, but whether the good Saivite
has all that he needs with his "grace" or his
religion and will not need to become a
Christian, or vice versa.[4]

Panikkar's current view about dialogue can
be found in The Intra-Religious Dialogue published in 1978. This book, a collection of his
articles about dialogue written in the 1970s,
also shows that for him, inter-religious dialogue
itself is a religious task, "a religious imperative and historical duty."[5] The present day world
faces plurality in everyday life. The meeting of
religions is inescapable. Panikkar says that one
principle should govern dialogue. That principle
is this: The Religious Encounter must be a truly
religious one. In his editorial in the Journal
of Ecumenism of Summer, 1974, he stated that "the
encounter and dialogue between religions, ideolo-
gies and Weltanschaungen is a human imperative of
our time.... This dialogue itself is a religious
endeavor."[6] Religious dialogue, being itself
religious, necessarily presupposes "a deep human
honesty in search for truth whenever it can be
found, an intellectual openness in this search
without bias or prejudice, and also profound
loyalty towards ones own religion."[7] In the
earlier works there seemed to be an emphasis on
objectivity rather than subjectivity. In the
article "Christianity and World Religions," which
was delivered as a lecture in 1968, he suggested
that it is possible to learn the Christian
attitude towards other religions by an objective
investigation of the basic principles of Christianity and its history and the theological
interpretation of both. In his earlier years he
was interested in the objective study of religion. In Religionen und die Religion (1965) he
attempted to work out the common structure of all

religions from an objective perspective. In his
later years he felt the need of a theology of
religion and philosophy of religion which can be
based on the subjective multi-religious experience.[8] In The Trinity and Religious Experience of
Man he indicates the co-relation of subjective
and objective.[9]

Panikkar thinks that because inter-religious
dialogue is a religious task and not a mere
intellectual enterprise, therefore "if Inter-religious dialogue is to be real dialogue, an
intra-religious dialogue must accompany it."[10] It
necessitates a self-critical attitude. It starts
with accepting the challenge of a change, of
upsetting one's old patterns, of being converted.
One has to have the attitude of Augustine: "I
have made a question of myself." Thus the convinced exclusivists or convinced inclusivists
cannot have a religious dialogue.

A self-critical attitude, however, does not
mean not being committed to one's own religious
convictions. Panikkar indicates the inadequacy
of "epoche" in the sphere of religious encounters. He says that "epoche" in the sphere of
religious encounter is psychologically impracti-
cable, phenomenologically inappropriate, philoso-
phically defective, religiously barren. "Epoche"
may be useful for having a phenomenological study
of religions--to gain information about them.
However, it is not genuine understanding of a
religion. In order to have genuine dialogue
there is need of understanding the partner of the
dialogue as she/he understands her or himself.
However, this cannot be achieved in the "neutral
dialectical arena."[11] Only those who have that
genuine commitment to their faith which indicates
that their religion is wide enough and deep
enough to embrace the other as self can understand the other as self. Thus only those can
understand the other religious tradition with
commitment as their own and engage in a genuine
religious dialogue. He gives the example of
Rāmkrishna Panamahamsa and Roberto de Nobili as
people who did enter into the heart of religions
other than their own while committed to their
own.[12]

Panikkar indicates that commitment and
openness can go together if the distinction
between faith and belief is kept in mind. Faith

3

is that which connects us with transcendence. It
is expressed in forms of ideas which is belief.
Faith is more than any particular formulation of
it in belief. However, it is always accompanied
by some form of belief. Beliefs are different.
They are not interchangeable. Yet they exhibit
the similarity of nature which makes dialogue
possible. He says: "They (beliefs) are gene-
rally equivalent in that every belief has a
similar function: to express Man's faith, that
faith which is the anthropological dimension
through which Man reaches his goal--in Christian
language, his salvation."[13] Thus the believers of
one tradition can be open to others as they know
that their faith is more than the doctrines that
they believe in and practices they follow.

Panikkar notes that because religious
dialogue involves risks--the risks of being
shaken from one's well formulated convictions, of
being converted--it is not possible for everyone
to engage in dialogue. As evangelist needs a
calling so also does religious dialogue. "Hardly
anyone would be equal to it but for the very
drive of faith that invites us to hazard our life
without fear, even to lose it."[14]

According to Panikkar dialogue is not simply
a methodology but essentially a religious act.
Therefore, it is not possible to prescribe any
formal rigid rules for it. It moves along as
long as it is done in a spirit of openness along
with commitment. However, he gives the example
of a Christian-Vaisnava dialogue to indicate how
it can move, and from which we perhaps can
develop some guidelines. Panikkar stated that a
Christian has to try to internalize the Vaisnava's experience of Krsna the best sheµhe can.
The Vaiṣṇava is the one who would judge the
authenticity of the Christian's experience of
Krsna. The Christian then tries to relate this
experience with his or her experience of Christ
and describe it to the partner of dialogue. The
Vaisnava also goes through the similar parallel
process. We shall quote Panikkar to indicate
what follows.

Here an alternative lies before me (Christian): Either I have ceased to be a Chris-
tian--belief in Krsna has supplanted my
belief in Christ, I have found a loftier,
fuller divine reality in Krsna than in

4

Christ--or else I am able to establish a special kind of bond between the two that both religions, or at least one of them, can acknowledge and accept (I do not say they already have accepted it).[15]

Similar possibilities are there for the Vaisnava.

From Panikkar's presentation we can say that the first requirement of dialogue is the attempt to realize the spiritual experience of the dialogue partner. This is what Monchanin called the adoption of the religion of the dialogue partner. This of course necessitates the learning of all the aspects of the partner's religious traditions, its culture, its emotional and historical associations, its myths and archetypes, its ideas and conceptual background. But the most fundamental element is the attitude with which it is done. It is not a simple intellectual effort but a religious one, not a determination of truth in intellectual terms, but an attempt to realize it in a way which enables authentic living. The second step of dialogue is the verification of the authenticity of this experience by the dialogue partner. The third step is integration of this new experience with the original experience. This integrated experience has to be acceptable to at least one of the traditions if not to both.

The results that would follow from dialogue cannot be predicted. However, insofar as in dialogue one listens and observes as well as speaks, one corrects as well as is corrected, it can be said that dialogue promotes mutual understanding; it implies growth and development. This is exemplified in Panikkar's own opinion about the aim and result of dialogue. In the early work The Unknown Christ of Hinduism he says that the aim of dialogue is to achieve unity. Here as a Christian he proposes to the Hindu dialogue partner: "Let us embrace one another and not keep aloof any longer, but merge into the oneness we desire, let us discover this unity, let us mix our waters and realize that identity you are convinced of and which we are striving for."[16] He seems to think that the two traditions cannot have their separate identity but merge into an unity. In his later work, he no longer thinks that dialogue is a means to convergence, although it might very well happen. Dialogue is

not a means of converting other, it is not a
means of gathering of information about the
other, but a way of coming to know and discover
oneself and, thus, grow together. In the introduction of the <u>Intra-Religious Dialogue</u> he writes
that,

> The aim of intra-religious dialogue is
> understanding. It is not to win over the
> other or to come to a total agreement or a
> universal religion. The ideal is communica-
> tion in order to bridge the gulfs of mutual
> ignorance and misunderstanding between the
> different cultures of the world, letting them
> speak and speak out their own insight in
> their own languages. Some may wish even to
> reach communion, but this does not imply at
> all that the aim is uniform unity or a
> reduction of all the pluralistic variety of
> Man into one single religion, system, ideo-
> logy or tradition.[17]

Panikkar indicates that pluralism is the factual
situation of the world. It should be taken
seriously. Cross-fertilization within this
pluralistic world leads to mutual fecundation.
The "two way traffic" between the different
traditions is needed for their vitality and
dynamism.

    Panikkar's view of dialogue indicates its
difference from comparative religion as well as
debate, from both of which it is not often
clearly distinguished. Comparative religion can
be a purely intellectual enterprize, dialogue
involves the total person and not simply his
intellect. However it has to emphasize the
intellect also to the extent that it is in the
sphere of speaking and listening and not in the
realm of silence of the mystical experience. In
order to speak in an intelligible manner it has
to have accurate conceptual formulations. The
feedback from the dialogue partner also comes
through speech and hence concepts. What distinguishes dialogue from comparative religion is the
attitude of mind. In comparative religion it is
possible to maintain intellectual aloofness,
whereas in dialogue involvement and emotional
risks of being shaken from the security of some
rigid doctrines of philosophies are the prerequi-
sites.

The attitude of mind is also the basic
difference between debate and dialogue. Both
involve commitment to truth. But in the case of
debate the person engaged in debate thinks that
he already knows what it is, whereas the person
involved in dialogue thinks he is still on the
way to truth. That is why in debate a person
tries to prove a point, but in dialogue one wants
to learn, re-evaluate and thus grow and develop.

Since dialogue is different from comparative
religion and debate, its requirements from them
also are different. For comparative religion and
debate intellectual ability is enough. For
dialogue spiritual depth is most fundamental. A
simple academician cannot be engaged in dialogue
if he or she is also not spiritually motivated.
Dialogue, however, has its academic value as
well. Comparative religion or phenomenological
study of religion can only provide some external
information about the different religious traditions of the world. They cannot promote insight
into the spiritual depth of the traditions.
Dialogue explores this spiritual depth and hence
can provide an understanding religious traditions
from the internal perspective. If dialogue is to
be differentiated from comparative religion and
debate, Panikkar's view of it as a religious act
demarcates it quite well as it highlights its
essential characteristics. However, when we look
at its requirements problems start to crop up.
The first step of dialogue according to Panikkar
is to try to understand the dialogue partner as
self. Whether and how far that is possible is
controversial. Some suggest (e.g., VanderLeew)
one cannot understand the other as long as one is
committed to his or her own faith. Others think
(Kristinson) that commitment to one's faith
enables one to have empathy for another tradition. The Catholics who are in dialogue with
Hinduism are not in agreement among themselves.
Whereas Abhisiktananda advocated "epoché,"
Klostermaier and Panikkar suggest conscious
commitment. It can, however, be said that if the
dialogue partner can be understood as self that
would be the ideal situation.

Similarly, with regard to the judgment of
the authenticity of the understanding and the
acceptability of the integrated experience to the
different traditions, the problem of criterion
seems to be a difficult one. Panikkar says that

the authenticity of the understanding of the partner's religious tradition is to be judged by the partner him/herself. However, if dialogue is to be a bridge between two traditions and not simply an exchange of opinion of two individuals, then the partners of the dialogue have to represent the community of their respective religious traditions. In the different religious traditions the criterion of authority is not the same. In the different schools of Hinduism, experience (anubhava) is considered the final criterion. However, when the experience is not yet achieved, Scripture (Brahma Sùtra 1.1.3) and the life and sayings of the saints are considered as authoritative. In Catholicism the Scriptures and the Church Tradition (past and present) are authoritative. The Scriptures in each tradition are not understood by all in the same way. In the case of Catholic Church what is condemned at one time may be accepted at another. In the case of Hinduism the determination of authenticity is even more difficult as there is no official body like Catholic Church. The question of authority is a difficult question in all traditions. Therefore, the judgement of the authenticity of the understanding by each other is a difficult one. We can however, agree with Panikkar insofar as he says that a Christian cannot claim that he understands Vaisṇavism better than a Vaisṇava nor can a Vaisṇava claim that he understands Christianity better than a Christian. For similar reasons to judge whether the integrated experience is acceptable to the different traditions is difficult. Panikkar suggests that at least partial authenticity would be sufficient. If the understanding and the integration of the experience is not totally strange and can be recognized at least in some strata of the traditions it would serve the purpose of dialogue. Some may fear that dialogue would bring total chaos. It is not an impossibility. Yet it is not anything more dangerous than the changes that are brought about by the internal factors operative within each tradition. The example of the Protestant movement in reaction to the factors (like selling of indulgences in the medieval Church) operative within the Church would be sufficient to illustrate the point. Dialogue is the present day need. The changes that may come through dialogue should not be considered more dangerous than the changes that may come from internal factors within each tradition.

8

Following Panikkar's own scheme, in the next chapter we shall present his understanding of Hinduism and try to determine how far this is acceptable to the various Hindu traditions.

Notes

Panikkar on Dialogue

[1] John Hick, ed., Truth and Dialogue in World Religions: Conflicting Truth Claims (Philadelphia: Westminster Press, 1974), would give an idea in what diverse way the term dialogue has been used.

[2] Hans Küng advocates dialogue. He thinks it is to be used to prove the supremacy of Christianity. Chapter 3 of his On Being a Christian (Garden City, N.Y.: Doubleday, 1974), would indicate it very clearly. Non-Christians would not be interested in this kind of dialogue. Panikkar, Klostermaier or most of the Catholics that we have mentioned in the introduction who are engaged in dialogue with Hinduism advocate dialogue with openness.

[3] Panikkar The Unknown Christ of Hinduism (London: Darton, Longman and Tod, 1964), p. 10.

[4] Ibid., p. 7.

[5] Panikkar, Intra-Religious Dialogue, (New York: Paulist Press, 1978), p. 40.

[6] Id., editorial note in Journal of Ecumenical Studies (Summer, 1974), p. 516.

[7] Id., Unknown Christ of Hinduism, p. 3.

[8] Id., The Intra-Religious Dialogue, chs. 2 and 3.

[9] Id., The Trinity and the Religious Experience of Man, p. 1-3.

[10] Id., Intra-Religious Dialogue, p. 50.

[11] Ibid., p. 41.

[12] Ibid., p. 41.

[13] Ibid., p. 22.

[14] Ibid., p. 13.

[15] Ibid., p. 14.

16 Id., _The Unknown Christ of Hinduism_, p. 21.

17 Id., _Intra-Religious Dialogue_, p. xxvii.

Chapter 2
Panikkar on Hinduism

Panikkar believes that in order to be in
dialogue with any tradition that tradition has to
be understood from the inside. One has to learn
about that tradition the way a child learns a
language, by associating words with objects, and
not the way an adult learns a foreign language,
by translation of each word to his own language.
This is the only authentic form of learning and
understanding. Whether a person committed to his
own faith can at the same time understand another
tradition as his own is controversial. Panikkar
believes that because the context of religious
experience of the present day world is global,
multi-religious experience is not only possible
for a few, but is going to be a more and more
recurrent phenomenon. In "multi-religious
experience" he wrote that, "I 'left' as a Christian; I 'found' myself a Hindu; and I 'return' as
a Buddhist; without having ceased to be Christian."[1] According to him, the basic forms of all
spirituality are "theandric" which is expressed
in Christianity in the form of Trinity and in
Hinduism in the form of bhakti, jñāna and karma.
Trinity is not the exclusive property of Christianity nor are karma, bhakti and jñāna the exclusive property of Hinduism. Panikkar says:

> The author, however, believes that he ex-
> presses not a private opinion, but a paradigm
> of an experience which is bound to become
> more and more frequent in our time: the
> experience of gathering or rather concentra-
> ting in oneself more than one phyla in which
> mankind's fundamental insights have accumula-
> ted.[2]

Panikkar's writings on Hinduism indicate
that he studies "the belief, the word, the
archetypes, the culture, the mystic and conceptual background, the emotional and historical
associations,"[3] which he thinks are essential for
understanding a religious tradition. He did not
simply skim through the different Hindu scriptures, which are so numerous, but attempted to
penetrate deeply into their hearts. His understanding is not a simple intellection but an
attempt of what the Hindus call anubhava, or

13

realization. Perhaps his Indian heritage was of advantage to him. However, all born Hindus are neither acquainted with nor do they go to the heart of their scriptures. With all his attempts of understanding Hinduism, Panikkar is still a Christian and therefore, his understanding of Hinduism is colored by his Catholic stance. This does not run counter to Panikkar's own model for bridge-building insofar as a Hindu can recognize his interpretation as "at least partially orthodox."[4] The different schools of Hinduism would not agree with all his interpretations but the partial authenticity of his interpretation also cannot but be recognized as we hope to indicate in this chapter. Panikkar wrote a few books comparing Hinduism and Christianity. He also wrote several books entirely on Hinduism.[5] Besides he has written more than one hundred articles in different journals about Hinduism and Christianity.

In his comparative works Panikkar tries to show the somewhat superior and exclusivistic character of the Christian Gospel. However, he understands Christian exclusivism in a very inclusivistic way. In the next chapter we shall see how broad it is and how his view is influenced by Hinduism. He does not attempt to prove the superiority of Christianity on the basis of history as Hans Küng does.[6] Rather he thinks that for the purpose of dialogue the historical dimension is not enough. Nor does he want to differentiate Hinduism and Christianity as "other worldly" and "this-worldly" as Albert Schweitzer does.[7] He does not think that there is an either/or relationship between Hinduism and Christianity. He believes that Christ is hidden in Hinduism and needs to be manifested. Therefore, his criticisms of Hinduism are about its partial-nature, its incompleteness, rather than an outright condemnation of Hinduism.

Criticism of Hinduism.

Panikkar in his writings often refers to certain inadequacies of Hinduism. However, in one of his works Misterio y Revelación, in the chapter, "The Crisis of Indian Philosophy," he has dealt with the problems of Hindu philosophy in the context of Murti's book The Central Philosophy of Buddhism. The thrust of his criticism is that spirituality cannot be a matter

of intellectual enterprise. He can agree with
Murti's contention that dialectic can be a
critique of reason. Without reference to
Buddha's enlightenment dialectic cannot assure
prajñá, or wisdom. Most Hindu theologians would
agree with Panikkar including Śamkara whose view
is considered close to Buddhism. In the commentary on Brahma Sùtra Śamkara said that we can
know that Brahman is the source of everything in
the world from the scriptural sources,[8] although
he maintains that ultimately only intuition can
give one final assurance. However, we do not
think that Murti intended to say that dialectic
alone can assure prajñá. Panikkar agrees with
Murti in maintaining that the entire philosophy
of India moves around the tension of àtma-Vàda
(permanence) and anàtma-Vàda (non-permanence).
Àtma-Vàda can be pluralistic, dualistic or
monistic. The intellectual culmination is
monism. Monism denies all change and movement.
It denies causality. Anàtma-Vàda also ends up in
a denial of all change and movement as there is
nothing to change and move. Anàtma-Vàda also
denies causality. Panikkar indicates that the
problem with both is that they make the criterion
of intellectual intelligibility the criterion of
reality. The intellectual antinomy involved in
causality does not prove that it is not real.
Besides, from the perspective of spirituality
denial of all change and movement is the denial
of the starting point of spirituality. Panikkar
thinks that this is one of the reasons for which
India did not progress in the worldly sphere.
Panikkar believes that advaita is the true spirit
of Hinduism which can deal with the question of
permanence and change better than any other
system. He believes that the notion of Trinity
can be loyal to the Hindu primacy of oneness,
which, being a dynamic unity and not a static
one, can act as the cause, as ground of all the
beings of the world. His criticism of Hinduism
thus is about some of its doctrinal formulations
but not about its inner spirituality.

Hinduism's Contribution

        Panikkar is conscious of certain inadequa-
cies of Hinduism. However, for the purpose of
dialogue he is more interested in what Hindu
spirituality can contribute to his Christian
spirituality. He prefers to describe the ultimate as "One" rather than as "Other" which

follows the Hindu Scriptures. In _Trinity and the Religious Experience of Man_,[9] he indicates how advaita can help to understand the relationships of the Trinity which are One and three at the same time. Again, the Hindu emphasis on the non-personal notion of the ultimate can be a corrective to Mediterranean Christian anthropomorphic idea of God. In _Los Dioses Y el Senor_ he gives a summary of what can be learned and reflected upon from Hinduism. 1.) There exists the possibility of a pluralism which does not imply falling in the trap of agnostic relativism. 2.) This pluralism, which is the ground of all tolerance gets its justification from the distinction between orthodoxy and orthopraxies. If. e.g., Christianity is identified with "Orthodoxy" then those who believe in a different doctrine have to be condemned. However, if Christianity is orthopraxies then those who with sincere faith act in a human cooperation can be considered to be participating in the same mystery that the Christians believe in. 3.) The pluralism of the doctrines results from the transcendence of the reality-truth and from the imperfections of human knowledge. 4.) The logical possibility and the vigor of one hermeneutic does not justify its existential truth. For this there is need for other criterion: from the Catholic perspective, the Church--others perhaps would say Scriptures and Tradition. 5.) The task of hermeneutics itself urges us to transcend it and indicate that this is not the only and definitive way to salvation. "In other words: the hermeneutic can be multiple, because there is no ultimate instance, because it must always be superceded, in life, in the being, in the faith, in the mystery."[10]

It is very much evident that Panikkar has a very positive view of Hinduism. However, this is dependent on the way that he understands the nature of Hindu spirituality. We shall therefore see how he understands Hinduism and investigate whether it can be justified from the perspective of the different traditions of Hinduism.

Interpretation of Hinduism

The Vedic Experience: Mantramanjari is the most voluminous text by Panikkar about Hinduism. It is an interpreted anthology of the Hindu Scriptures, the Vedas. However, the purpose of

16

this book is not an exposition of Hinduism, nor exegesis of the Vedas according to Hindu traditions, nor an analysis of it in terms of Western categories as the Western Indologists do. The subtitle "An Anthology of the Vedas for Modern Man and Contemporary Celebration," indicates the broad perspective from which this book is written. In the general introduction of this book Panikkar writes:

It is an account of the Vedic Revelation, understood as unveiling of depths that still resound in the heart of Modern Man, so that he may become more conscious of his own human heritage and thus of the springs of his own being.[11]

According to Panikkar any true spirituality is theandric in nature. Therefore, any proper religious scripture would indicate this theandrism. The Vedas, containing the wisdom of India, is a truly religious scripture. Hence, it is theandric. Panikkar arranges his whole anthology to bring out the theandrism of the Vedas. This can be illustrated from the first section of part IV--The Ascending Way. Panikkar writes: "No kind of dualism or plurality can be the lasting and final foundation of all."[12] However, this is not to be understood in a monistic way.

We witness three moments of one and the same ultimate process: the _divine_ giving himself up so as to be able to produce the world out of himself; the cosmos coming and exploding into beings ... man discovering the all-encompassing One and finding the same time a place for himself in the _advitiya_ of the oneness.[13]

This is very similar to Panikkar's theandric interpretation of the Christian Trinity: Father--Non-Being, Son--Being, Spirit--the return of the Being.[14]

Panikkar himself writes about the purpose of this book:

This book aims, insofar as possible, at being free from all peculiar preconceptions and particular value judgments. The Sruti must be rescued from the monopoly of a single

17

group of pundits and indologists or an active
religio-political faction.[15]

Although he is saying that the presentation is
without any value judgment, yet he is polemical
about the Hindu scholastic interpretation of the
Vedas as well as the interpretations of the
Western Indologists. Thus it is a two-pronged
battle to rescue the Srùti from the exclusive
interpretation and misinterpretation. It is an
ambitious and fascinating venture. According to
Panikkar Hindu spirituality is not monistic,
pantheistic or polytheistic-it is advaitic or
non-dualistic. Therefore, Panikkar interprets
all the identity statements of the Vedas and
Upanisads in a non-monistic way. This book gives
some insight about Panikkar's understanding of
Hinduism. However, for a systematic exposition
of Hinduism we have to rely chiefly on his work,
"Algunos Aspectos de la Spiritualidad Hindu." The
work attempts to give an insight about Hindu
spirituality to the Western Christian readers.
Here, however, he often relates the points of
similarity between Hinduism and Christianity and
makes a few oblique remarks about the monistic
tendencies of Hinduism. He seems to be particularly unhappy with the neo-Vedántins, the chief
representatives of which are Vivekánanda and the
monks of Rámakrishna order.[16] However, the
purpose of this book is not a criticism of
Hinduism but an exposition of Hinduism from his
in-depth understanding of it. He wants his
Christian readers to have a sympathetic view of
Hinduism and thus sometimes it betrays a
pro-Hindu apologetic note. Nevertheless, his
exposition of Hinduism shows that his understanding is very much colored by his Christian
stance.

In the preface of this work Panikkar states
that it is impossible to give a summary of the
centuries of wisdom of the spirituality of a good
part of humanity within the range of a few
hundred pages.[17] Besides, Hinduism and Christianity are not homogeneous. Thus there is always
the danger of misunderstanding and distortion,
even with the best possible intention and honesty. Again, because the Western mentality is
different from the Indian mentality it is difficult to write about Hinduism for the Westerners.
He proposes to present Hinduism in two parts.
The first part is descriptive. He gives a sketch

of the history of Hindu spirituality. The second
part he calls as positive and not critical. It
attempts to deal with what he thinks to be some
fundamental aspects of Hindu spirituality.

In the introduction Panikkar tries to
explain some of the technical terms like Hinduism
and spirituality. Since Radhakrishnan, all
textbooks on Hinduism usually start with an
explanation of the term "Hinduism." Panikkar's
explanation of it is interesting from methodolo-
gical perspective. To indicate what Hinduism is,
he follows the Hindu method of ontological
reduction by stating what it is not. He says:

> Hinduism is not a doctrine (can as such have
> many Hindu doctrines), not an idea (hence
> does not have the necessity of logical
> coherence), not an organization, not a rite.
> Hinduism does not have a limit. It does not
> have definition. If anything is self-evi-
> dently "true," Hindus would immediately
> accept it as their own. The greatest fear of
> Hinduism is that truths (partial) destroy the
> Truth (total).

According to Panikkar Hinduism cannot be understood by reason only. "Hinduism demands a
conversion of the factic-order of the mere
existence in order to be understood."[19] Hinduism
desires to be the "Truth," and as such does not
want to give one particular content to that
"Truth." Any intellectual truth limits itself and
excludes others. "Hinduism for its respect of
"Truth" admits everything in the logical
sphere."[20] Panikkar does not imply, as Poussen
does, that Indians are innocent of the law of
contradiction.[21] What he means is that according
to the Hindu traditions "Truth" transcends all
intellectual formulation of it. Hence in Hinduism the emphasis is not on "orthodoxy," rather it
is on "praxis." In the intellectual sphere,
though the need of logical consistency is emphasized, as it is evident from the detailed description of logical fallacies in Nyàya logic, in
using non-contradiction as a criterion of logical
consistency in Màdhyamika kàrikà of Nàgàrjuna and
Brahmasùtra Bhàsys of Śamkara, yet it is recognized by the Hindus that ''Truth" is beyond any
intellectual formulation of it. Therefore, in
Hinduism anathema itself is anathema.

19

Panikkar says that if Hinduism is to be
called by any name, it should be named as Sanātana Dharma, the perennial order. Dharma, which
had been translated in varied terms as religion,
ordination, duty, rule, correctness, morality,
custom, law, virtue, merit, etc. would be the
true nature of Hinduism. This is most fundamental for Hinduism. Panikkar makes his oblique
remarks about the neo-Vedāntins by saying that
they distort Hinduism by calling it Hindu Dharma.
Any dharma insofar as it is Dharma would be
Hindu. However, the neo-Vedāntins use of the
term is only a concessation to the Western use of
the term. Panikkar indicates that according to
its etymological origin from the root dhr which
means "to take," "to bear" and according to the
description of Mahābhārata as well, dharma means
that which maintains, that which forebears the
people. Panikkar thinks that the best translation of the word would be "order" in the Medieval
Scholastic ontological sense of the term. There
exists a real ontological order in this world,
not simply in the sense of order in the external
objects of nature, but in its most fundamental
ontic structure. Panikkar says that this order,
which sometimes appears as personified
(Mahābhārata) to give it better consistency and
life, represents the ontic hierarchical structure
of being.[22] Denial of it is self-denial; guarding
it one reaches the plenitude of life. Knowledge
of this order is ultimate and salvific wisdom.
This order regulates cosmos, individual as well
as social. Morality and all the other positive
values are values insofar as they are expressions
of this order.

    Panikkar says that one fundamental concept
of Hinduism is Svadharma, i.e., the personal
dharma of one's own. Everyone has an ontic
position in the scale of beings. The greatest
obligation of a Hindu is to follow hisūher own
dharma, i.e., the law which regulates the development of hisū her existence and it is converted
into duty. In this way the harmony of this
totality is maintained.[23]

    The ontological nature of dharma explains
what is known as reincarnation in Hinduism.
Panikkar does not agree with the popular interpretation of reincarnation as the body-hopping of
a permanent soul. Rather it signifies continuity. There has to be continuity to guarantee the

possibility of correcting the disorders of the
bad action of humans as well as the disorder of
nature. Otherwise, there would be chaos. Ontological atomism means destruction of being.
"There must be continuity: the samsàra, the
Cycle of the existences."[24] Panikkar's interpretation of reincarnation is very close to the
Buddhist interpretation of it. His interpretation can do justice to the Hindu idea of collec-
tive karma, showing the ontological interdepen-
dence of all beings.

Panikkar makes a distinction between Dharma
and religion. Dharma refers to being, whereas
religion is the different ways and doctrines that
unite us with our end (our being). Religion is
the means by which humans reach their ends. This
implies knowledge and practice. If humans do not
know and cannot practice a way which leads them
to their end they would be un-religious. They
cannot be adhàrmic as Dharma is the reality of
their being and cannot be denied, whether it is
recognized or not. Thus human actions can be
adhàrmic but the humans themselves cannot be so.
Dharma can be realized in many ways. Each being
possesses his/her own dharma. "Religion is the
Svadharma concretized by a person or a group."[25]
Panikkar thinks that this idea is at the root of
Hindu tolerance. Hindu tolerance is about
religion--about doctrines. However, as far as
Dharma is concerned it cannot be tolerant as it
is the basis of all tolerance. It does not and
cannot deny the existence of the indestructible,
unchangeable ontic order which leaves open the
possibility of diverse interpretations of it.
Panikkar indicates that Hinduism insists, above
all, on the act of faith but leaves the question
of the object of faith open. "That which is
important is not an 'idea.' the content, the
formulation of the creed; but the act of belie-
ving."[26]

Panikkar indicates that as for Hinduism
dharma is more important than religion, so also
spirituality is more important than religion.
Spirituality carries individuals to their goals.
Spirituality in this sense has a certain independence from dogma although some form of dogma
would always accompany any form of spirituality.
This implies that the same dogma can serve
different forms of spirituality and different
dogmas can give rise to the same form of spiritu-

21

ality. As an example of the former he refers to
the Benedictine and Franciscan orders. For the
latter he refers to Buddhist and Christian
monasticism. Panikkar thinks that this relative
independence of spirituality from dogma enables
him to deal with certain fundamentals of Hindu
spirituality without referring to its different
dogmas. This also would enable the Christian
readers to stop making hasty conclusions about
Hinduism. Panikkar does not deal with the Hindu
philosophical schools of thought; rather he deals
with the practical aspects of the Hindu doctrines.

        The first part of the essay deals with the
historical development of Hinduism. Panikkar
thinks that a historical survey of Hinduism is
almost next to impossible. Any form of Hinduism
or any particular period of Hinduism has within
itself so many currents and influences that a
simple bi-dimensional (space-time) account cannot
do justice to it. However, Panikkar attempts to
divide Hinduism in some time periods. In his
division he follows the classical Hindu way of
doing its history according to predominance of
some scriptures, rather than the occidental way
of dividing the history of any religious tradition into ancient, medieval and modern. First,
is the pre-Vedic period, which he dates from 3000
to 2000 B.C. Then follows the period of Srùti
(revelation). Under this period there is the
period of Vedic spirituality (approximately
2000-1000 B.C.) and the period of Upanisadic
spirituality (1000-600 B.C.). The period of
Srùti is followed by the period of Smrti (tradition). Within this period there is the following: a) the period of reaction to the schisms
of Buddhism and Jainism. This is the period of
the Vendàngas and Kalpasùtras, which lasted from
600 to 300 B.C. This can also be called the
period of Dharma Sàstra. Panikkar designates
Buddhism and Jainism as Schisms. Whereas many
Hindu scholars, e.g., Radhakrishnan would agree
with him,[27] the Buddhist scholars think them to
be new religions. Panikkar himself in Mysterio y
Revelación criticized Prof. Murti for not recognizing the radical difference between Hinduism
and Buddhism.[28] b) The period of epics in the
Itihàsa (History) (300 B.C.- 300 A.D.); c) the
period of Myths or early Purànas (perhaps from
6th century B.C. to 3rd century A.D.). The
period of Smrti was followed by the period of

22

Bhāsyas (commentaries). This period includes:
a) the period of darśanas (philosophical schools)
from 300 A.D.-700 A.D.; b) the period of Āgamas
or the great religions of Hinduism (700 A.D.-1400
A.D.). These schools started from the time of
Purānas; c) the popular spiritualities which
perhaps can be characterized by the predominance
of bhakti (from 1400 A.D.-1750 A.D); d) the
period of modern reforms (1750 A.D.-1950). It
started with the time of a certain renaissance
from the Islamic period and then followed all the
movements which led to the independence of India.

In the division of Hinduism different time
periods Panikkar presented a neat scheme.
However, because scholarship is not unanimous
about the dates of the different scriptures, it
should be mentioned that the dates are approxi-
mate and are not to be understood as conclusive.
Within the confines of twenty-one pages, however,
Panikkar presents a clear and quite accurate
picture of the different periods of Hinduism. He
pointed out that what is known as Hinduism is a
development from very varied and complex factors
of pre-Vedic-pre-Aryan and Vedic-Aryan India. He
shows his insight into the nature of Srùti
(revelation) by comparing it with Quranic and
Christian idea of revelation. "While the Quran,
from the perspective of Orthodox Islam, contains
the revelation of God to Man, while Bible nar-
rates the events and salient sayings of the
Revealer, directly in (NT) or indirectly (OT),
the Srùti is Revelation itself."29 The Vedas are
the conceptual presentation of the Srùti. Srùti
is not a doctrine or dogma. It has to be
listened to and realized.

In the first section of the essay when
Panikkar presents the history of Upanisdic
spirituality, his presentation is theistic. As
in The Vedic Experience, here also, he explains
the identity statements of the Upaniṣads in a
theistic way. The message of Upaniṣad and
Hinduism in general, according to Panikkar, is
not monism but non-dualism which is not incompatible with theism in general and Christianity in
particular.

In the second half of the essay Panikkar
deals with what he thinks to be certain fundamental aspects of Hindu spirituality. He describes
the religious character of the caste-system, the

23

four stages of life and the four goals of life of
Hinduism. He describes the salient features of
Vaiṣṇavism, Śaivism and Tāntrism. Because, as
Panikkar has indicated, Hinduism is more practical than theoretical, the spiritual paths
(Mārgas) are very important. We shall discuss
Panikkar's presentation of the three mārgas
(ways) of Hinduism to indicate his double loyal-
ty-- loyalty to what he considers to be the true
spirit of Hinduism as well as loyalty to what he
considers to be the true spirit of Christianity.

    The Bhāgavad Gitā describes the three ways
of spirituality Karma (action) Jñāna (knowledge)
and Bhakti (devotion). The different Hindu
thinkers according to their different leanings
tend to emphasize one or the other of these ways.
Panikkar thinks that the Bhaktiyoga is the most
comprehensive including the other two. Here, he
shows his Christian preference.

    According to Panikkar the way that is to be
followed is related to how the goal or end is
understood. If it is understood as the Real then
the way is karma and the fundamental category is
sacrifice. If the goal is understood as the
Truth--then the way is jñāna and the fundamental
category is gnosis. If the end is understood as
Good then the way is bhakti and the fundamental
category is person.

    Its (goods) acquisition demands an absolute
    surrender and consecration, total devotion to
    the good. Only pure and disinterested love
    can lead to Him. The good is not a mere
    value but a Person. We have here the bhakti
    mārga or the way of devotion. Its fundamen-
    tal category is person and love is its
    quintessence.³⁰

    Good possesses two intimately connected
aspects: the Good properly speaking as the
transcendental object of the will and the Beauty
as the goal of sentiment. They always go together. Therefore, they, in the end form one
single way. A Good that is not Beautiful cannot
be loved, a Beauty that is not Good cannot be
desired. Thus within the bhakti mārga two
tendencies can be discerned: the bhakti of pure
love, due to the influence of the way of knowledge and the love of the Beauty due to the
influence of the way of karma. The first follows

24

an intellectual and transparent love of the Good
without any quality or attribute. The second
follows a totally integrated, solid and sentimen-
tal love towards the Good and does not allow any
separated and atomistic existence. Tàntrism
developed this form of bhakti to its maximum
limit.

Panikkar not only believes in the comprehensive nature of the bhakti yoga, he seems also
to believe in an evolution from karma to jñàna
and ultimately to bhakti yoga. However, he
mentioned in other places the integrality of the
three màrgas. In his explanation of karma màrga
he says that karma can save insofar it is ontic,
i.e., it can give being to humanity.

This would be the same principle of the
evolution and even abandonment of the karmic
spirituality by the other two ways ... the
true activity which makes man (gives him his
authentic being) is knowledge,...; the real
action which makes man drink from the source
of Being itself and as such to participate
Him and receive his Being itself is devotion,
the love....[31]

Panikkar is not the only Catholic thinker who
believes in the supremacy and ultimacy of bhakti
Some other Catholics who are in dialogue with
Hinduism believe the same, e.g., R. C. Zaehner.
However, whereas Zaehner thinks that bhakti in
Hinduism can be considered a result of Christian
influence,[32] Panikkar believes that this is a
process within Hinduism itself. This is in
accordance with his thesis that Christ is already
hidden in Hinduism.

Panikkar indicates that karma, which is
usually translated as action, does not mean just
any kind of action. Action which is liturgic
i.e., theandric, is implied by the karma màrga.
Panikkar brings out very clearly the emphasis on
both pravrtti (involvement) and nivrtti
(non-attachment) in Hinduism. He says that it is
true that in some schools of Hinduism there seems
to be an exclusive emphasis on nivrtti. Therefore, Schweitzer's criticism of Hinduism as
otherworldly has some justification. However,
there are schools which emphasize pravrtti also.
Karma yoga as is taught in the Bhàgavad Gìtà is
the reconciliation of pravrtti and

nivrtti--action and contemplation. Panikkar
indicates that the Bhāgavad Gitā teaches Karma as
Naiskarma. It is neither inactivity nor mere
activity.

Inactivity cannot produce freedom from
action, northe renunciation of action by the
same token, carry one to his perfection.
Besides, it is not even physically possible.
Actually action can have value only when it
is done as a sacrifice.[33]

The Vedic idea of sacrifice brings out the
liturgic nature of the action. This also justifies the exegesis of the critics of simple
action. Action should not be done even for the
desire of salvation. Nothing can be done to save
oneself. However, the activity should go on till
the end for the maintenance of the world. God's
example supplies the supreme moral principle. It
consists in performance of action that must be
done without attachment to its fruits, actions
performed with divine mastery for the maintenance
of the world, without being bound by it or being
dependent on it. Man must comply with his duty
and be free from egotism which crops up immedi-
ately after a good deed is done.

Panikkar's interpretation of karma mārga is
in agreement with the interpretation of the
bhakti schools. The jñāni interpret it diffe-
rently. Karma can be performed by way of discrimination between the real and the unreal. The
ātman is really unaffected by actions which
belongs to the realm of prakrti, the ever active
energy of the world, or to the realm of māyā.
Panikkar, due to his Christian stance, explains
karma yoga as action dedicated to God. Panikkar
interprets the Gitā sayings that the individual
(ātman) is not the doer of action in an ingenious
way to show its congruence with Christianity. He
points out that the Gitā says that only God is
the performer of all genuine activity:

This action is a true theandric activity:
the man offers his action to God, but it is
God who accepts them and at bottom it is God
who performs them.[34]

In Le Mystere Du Culte where he tries to
bring out the significance of cultic action,
Panikkar goes even a step further in saying that

26

all authentic action is the operation of Christ. He says that the cult is "opus Dei," work of God, or more accurately "opus Christi," that is to say, theandric action, work at once divine and human.[35] Panikkar thinks that the karma yoga as is taught in the Gità is in agreement with the Christian teaching that humans cannot be saved by their own work (Gal 2: 16; Eph. II,9; Roman III 20, etc.) though they must be active (Lk 17:10) and good works are naturally done by a spiritual person because faith without action is death (Jn 2:20).[36]

Panikkar's analysis of jñāna yoga is explicitly Christian. He indicates that jñāna is gnosis divested of its heretical characteristics. It is not merely intellectual or conceptual knowledge. It is that wisdom which enables one to realize that Reality which is realized by karma yoga in an external and physical manner. The salvific quality of the sacrifice does not consist of the external activity but of the inner attitude. This attitude is Sraddhà or faith. According to Panikkar, faith is the salient point of jñāna yoga. If jñāna is disassociated from faith, then it becomes a mere intellectual enterprise and loses its soteriological value. He believes that certain Hindu thinkers fell into this trap. The greatest advocate of jñāna yoga, Samkara, in order to avoid this danger, always associated jñāna yoga with bhakti.[37] Panikkar indicates that the requisites for jñāna yoga show that it is not a merely intellectual enterprise. The requirements described by the different schools of Hinduism are as follows: a) Mumuk-sutva or desire for salvation, which is the source of Brahma-jijñāsà or the desire to know Brahman; b) Nityānitya-vastu-viveka or àtmanàtmà-vastuviveka i.e., the discrimination between what is real (àtman) and what is unreal (anàtman); c) Ihàmutraphala bhogaviràga or renunciation of fruits of action here and here-after; d) Sàdhana or cultivation of the fundamental virtues which according to Hindu traditions are six in number: (i) Sam or serenity and equanimity, (ii) dam or sense control, (iii) uparati or renunciation, (iv) titiksà or patience and forbearance, (v) Sasmàdhàna or mental concentration and (vi) Sraddhà or faith. Panikkar says that these requirements show that jñāna yoga requires a radical conversion which is not simply psychological but also moral and finally ontolo-

27

gical. Our worldly (laukika) existence is
transformed from phenomenal order (Vyāvahārika)
to the nominal (para-mārthika) order.[38] This is
justified from the Upaniṣadic sayings that the
ātman cannot be searched by the external sense
organs but is to be realized within the "city of
nine (Svetasvatara Up III 18; Gitā V. 13) or
eleven (Katha Up V.1) doors." Again, no one can
realize ātman if sheúhe did not abandon all the
evil ways and is not serene and prepared and not
with mental peace. (Brhadaranyaka Up Iv, 19, 23;
Mund up III; 1, 5; III, 1, 8).[39] Thus the true
jñāna or gnosis is not the result of a syllogism
nor can it be achieved by the power of our
intellect. Here in lies the compatibility of
grace and jñāna[40] as he believes that human
beings moral perfection is not possible by his
own effort only.

     Panikkar's presentation of jñāna yoga
insofar as it indicates its difference from a
merely intellectual enterprise is quite accurate
from the different Hindu perspectives. He
himself provides enough evidence from the Hindu
scriptures to justify his view. However, his
translation of Sraddhā as faith, his identification of jñāna with sacrifice in the sense of
theandric action and his reference to grace
without any further qualification are due to his
Christian presuppositions. It is true that the
great advaitin Saṁkara was himself a bhakta
(devotee) and jñāna yoga can and often is combined with bhakti yoga by many Hindus (e.g.,
Rāmakrishna). However, it can be practiced
independently from any theistic stance. In that
respect jñāna of Hinduism is closer to nonthe-
istic Buddhism than theistic Christianity. It is
considered a difficult path (like walking on the
edge of a razor). It has its pitfalls but so do
all the other ways of spirituality.

     Panikkar gives a detailed description of
bhakti yoga and does not hide his preference for
this over other ways. He says that this is the
better known and most popular of all the yogas.
If from the theoretical perspective some Hindus
consider jñāna yoga the most elevated one, yet in
practice bhakti does have primacy not simply in
popular religiosity but also in elaborated
theology. This can be called Hindu religion in
the Semitic occidental sense of the term. Bhakti
as a cult can be compared to karma and jñāna.

As karma is sacrificial rite and jñāna is sacrifice of the intellect, bhakti as the anthropological cult per-excellence is the sacrifice of this total human being. "Devotion" implies a return of the creature to the absolute. This absolute accepts the devotee and is sensitive to him. Bhāgavat Purāna states that God says, "I am the slave of my servants." Bhakti, as its etymology indicates, involves an active as well as a passive aspect. God loves and communicates Himself, the devotee adores and participates in the divine love. It is as much a divine gift as it is human adoration.

According to Panikkar the most fundamental requirement for bhakti mārga is the preparation and adoration of the devotee. An accurate conception of the Bhagavān ("Lord") is not needed. It does not mean that it should not be and is not attempted. The philosophies of Śamkara, Rāmānuja, Madhva, Nimbārka, Madava and Chaitanya combined bhakti with speculative philosophy. Although theism would seem to be the most adequate background for bhakti in India it can be combined with jñāna or even with idolatry. Love and dedication are its most important necessities. Panikkar indicates that Hindu devotion, as is represented in its different forms, and all of which can be classified under the two categories haituki (love for some reason) and ahaituki (pure love), has two variants in Hinduism, viz., naked love and nakedness of love. The naked love aspires only for God and abandons everything else, even himself. This coincides with jñāna yoga and soon becomes rigid advaita. The second, is the nakedness of love which is proper bhakti yoga. It converts everything by love and abandons nothing, as in reality there is no one to renounce and nothing to be renounced. Everything is transformed and purified by the fire of love. Its most typical example is to utilize human love as an example of and aid to understanding divine love.

Panikkar believes that because of the basic mystical quality of Hinduism the three mārgas cannot be kept separate from each other. The Hindus try to indicate their unity. Some new-Hindus (e.g., Vivekānada) try to bring these three together in a gradual order-starting with karma, going through bhakti and ending, in jñāna. Panikkar thinks that this is due to Western

influence. To be true to the genuine Hindu
spirit it is better to follow the Bhàgavad Gità
which calls them yogas (i.e., those which unite
us to our ends) and compare them with the different strands of one rope.

Panikkar indicates that in description of
the ultimate, in Hinduism there seems to be a
primacy of Oneness rather than describing it in
terms of Goodness, Truth and Existence. This, he
thinks, is to maintain the ineffability and
infinitude of the ultimate. No human categories,
nothing of the world, can describe the ultimate.
This is the reason for which God is described as
an "other" is West. Panikkar thinks that "other"
is a more appropriate description for the creatures than for God as the creatures are so only
in relationship to God and not vice versa.
Christianity, being associated with Western
philosophy which is in quest for Being, often
identified God with Being. This might serve the
purpose of intellectual intelligibility, but not
of the depth of spirituality. God is beyond the
description of all human catagories. Although
the primacy of oneness in Hinduism has its
advantages, Panikkar indicates that it has its
pitfalls as well. It is not capable of dealing
with the contingent, the point of departure,
i.e., the created realm. Ultimately the created
realm vanishes as "illusion." This is developed
in the philosophical schools of Màdhyamika,
Vijñànavàda and advaita-Vedànta. Panikkar is
critical of these schools of thought insofar as
anyone belonging to these schools does not take
the world seriously. He does not refer to any
classical member belonging to these schools by
name to criticize them. Rather he says that the
classical advaitin Śamkara is not an illusionist.
He is more critical of the modern Hindu thinkers,
for example, Vivekànanda for advocating a hierarchy of spirituality, and Murti for advocating
the idea that dialectic can lead to prajña.
Panikkar's criticisms of Vivekànanda and Murti,
although not totally unjustified, can be ques-
tioned. It is true that in Vivekànanda's writings there is an emphasis on jñàna. It is
mostly to counteract ritualism and the anthropomorphic idea of God that prevailed in his time
among many Hindus. Many instances of his life
indicate that he did not consider jñàna to be
superior to bhakti. He considered the
whole-hearted devotion of simple unsophisticated

men and women to be the peak of spirituality.
Again, in The Central Philosophy of Buddhism
Murti shows how dialectic helps prajñā. However,
he did not indicate that dialectic alone can lead
to prajñā. The purpose of Murti's book is not to
show how one attains nirvāna but to show how
mādhyamika philosophy as advocated by Nāgārjuna
justifies Buddha's silence about the avyākritas.
The spirit of Panikkar's criticisms however, is
undeniable. If any system of thought in the
field of religion overemphasizes the intellect
and in the process of explaining the world
explains it away, it is not acceptable. Among
the Hindu thinkers there are instances like
that--sri Harṣa or Prakāsānanda Sarasvati belong
to the school of advaita Vedānta. From
Panikkar's perspective understanding Hinduism and
trying to learn from it is more important than to
be overcritical of it. Therefore, to investigate
the accuracy of this understanding is more
important than to find out about the accuracy of
his criticism of any particular Hindu thinker.

Evaluation of Panikkar's understanding of Hinduism

        Here we encounter the problem of criterion.
Hinduism is the blanket name for diverse and
sometimes even contradictory traditions.
Panikkar referred to some of these diverse
traditions. He tried to understand and present
that understanding of Hinduism in some general
terms. Although generalities are often suspect
and Panikkar himself is aware of the fact that it
may emphasize the universal at the expense of the
concrete, yet it is unavoidable. If anything is
considered a general characteristic of the
diverse traditions, it should be true of all of
them. Panikkar's presentation of Hinduism as
theistic, non-dualistic, and his emphasis on
bhakti can not be justified according to this
criterion. Within Hinduism there are definite
non-theistic trends, for example, advaita of sri
Harṣa. Within Hinduism there are advocates of
dualism, for example, Madhva. Again according to
Panikkar's own understanding there are Hindus who
emphasize jñāna, for example Vivekānanda. If
Panikkar says that they misrepresent Hinduism,
then he is claiming he understand Hinduism better
than a Hindu, which runs counter to his own
proposed criterion that the authenticity of the
understanding of the dialogue partner's tradition

is to be judged by the partner. The problem of criterion very clearly shows the problem of dialogue between Hinduism and Catholicism in general. This also highlights the problem of any dialogue between any two traditions in general terms. Many religionists who are actively involved in dialogue are aware of this difficulty and indicate that a dialogue is possible only between two individuals. Panikkar in his example of a Hindu-Christian dialogue referred to the encounter between a <u>Vaisnava</u> and a Catholic. For the purpose of bridge-building between two traditions, this encounter is to be more than an encounter between two individuals. Panikkar is aware of this difficulty. He has an existential approach. He indicates that dialogue happens out of the necessities of time. Therefore, instead of formulating any rigid rule or criterion, it is practical to be flexible. Instead of hoping to reach any general agreement he proposes partial authenticity as sufficient for the purpose of dialogue. According to this criterion Panikkar's understanding of Hinduism need not be acceptable to all the Hindu traditions, but if it is recognized to be Hindu by some of them it would serve the purpose of dialogue. This criterion of partial authenticity can be justified from the perspective of Hinduism also. Although the different schools of Hinduism vie with each other to prove that their way of formulation of truth is the most adequate, all the Hindus believe in the inadequacy of intellectual formulation of truth. Therefore, adhering to any particular form of doctrine is not mandatory for the Hindus. In Hinduism there is nothing like being excommunicated from the society for holding on to some heresy. Therefore, if Panikkar's Christian understanding of Hinduism is not totally different from all the Hindus, it can be considered authentic.

According to this criterion of partial authenticity it can be easily indicated that Panikkar's Christian understanding of Hinduism is Hindu. All the <u>Shāktas</u>, <u>Śaivas</u> and <u>Vaisnavas</u> are theists if not monotheists as the Christians. The idea of God as is presented in Bhāgavat Purāna of <u>vaisnavism</u> is close to Christian understanding of God. This perhaps is the reason that the Christian, Klostermaier, could easily relate to the <u>Vaisnava</u> of <u>Vrindāvana</u>. Panikkar also refers to the <u>Vaisnava</u>. Sri Chaitanya's disgust about

the illusionists is not less than Panikkar. As a
Vaiṣṇava he believes in the universality of God's
saving power. God saves all--the ignorant, the
non-believer, the followers of foreign religions.
However, the māyāvādi of Venarasa evaded even
this all-compassing grace![41] Similarly it can be
said that Hinduism is non-dualistic. Not only
the advaita vedāntins but the Vaiṣṇavas who
advocate a personalistic relationship between God
and the devotee are primarily non-dualists.
According to Sri Critanya:
"panca-tattva-eka-vastu, nahi kichu bheda/rasa
asvadite tabu vividha vibheda."[42] (Spiritually
there is no difference between these five
tattvas, but to taste varieties distinctions are
made.) Panikkar's emphasis on bhakti also can be
justified from the perspectives of Śāktaism
Śaivism and particularly from Vaiṣṇavism.
According to Śāktaism total surrender to the
Mother is a way of salvation. It is evident from
the songs of Rāmaphrasāda. The Shaiva Siddhānta
school of Shaivism teaches that pashu, or humans,
can be free from their pāsha or fetters by the
grace of pati or the lord. For humans therefore,
there is one way to salvation, love and surrender
to the will of the lord. Viasnavism also teaches
the importance of devotion. Śri Chitanya was a
sanyāsi. Yet he did not spend his time in
studies of vedānta, but in praise and song about
God, as is mentioned again and again in
Sri-Caitanya-charitāmrta. In this age humans can
be saved by grace alone and by chanting the holy
name alone.[43]

    In the history of modern Hinduism
Rāmakrishna Paramahamsa is a universally recog-
nised important personality. His disciples
consider him as God-Incarnate. Most modern
Hindus even, if they may not have this extreme
veneration for him, recognize him as a saint.
His teaching, "there are as many ways to God as
there are different views," has become almost
like a dogma for many modern Hindus. He not only
influenced the thinking of the modern Hindu
thinkers he also influenced the thinking about
the relationships among different religions in
general. Panikkar himself considers him as an
ecumenist. Hindus consider life and saying of
saints as criterion of truth. Therefore, to find
out if Panikkar's understanding of Hinduism can
be justified from his perspective can be useful.

33

Rámakrishna was not a philosopher or scholar. As a matter of fact he was almost illite-
rate. His knowledge of the Hindu scriptures or
any other scripture, for example, the Bible, was
through others. He consequently made factual
mistakes in his references to them. Panikkar is
justified in saying that for Hinduism accurate
formulation of doctrine is not as important as
leading a spiritual life. This is exemplified in
Rámakrishna. In many of his conversations he
again and again indicated the limitation of what
he used to refer to as mere book knowledge.
Scriptures are to be studied to learn about the
ways by which God can be realized. He referred
to the sage who has a book with him containing
nothing but the name of Ráma. That was enough
for leading a spiritual life. He used to say it
is not really necessary to know all the factual
statements that are in the Gítá. If one gets its
essence that is enough. He used to say that the
essential teaching of the Gítá can be known by
repeating the name quickly for a few times.
Repeated in quick succession it sounds like Ta-gi
which means one who has renunciation and dis-
passion.44 Rámakrishna did not systematically
formulate any theology. His views are primarily
recorded in the Gospel of Sri Rámakrishna. This
book can easily justify Panikkar's understanding
of Hinduism. Rámakrishna speaks of God as
nirguna--attributeless, impersonal. He also
speaks of God as saguna--with attributes, personal.

> The term "Brahman" refers to that aspect of
> Divinity which is impersonal and which is
> beyond all activity. But when we think of
> Him as creating preserving and destroying all
> phenomena, then we call Him the Personal God,
> Divine Mother or Kali.
> In reality there is no distinction
> between "Brahman," or the Impersonal Abso-
> lute, and "Śakti," the Divine Mother. The
> Brahman and the Śakti are one just as fire
> and its burning power are one.45

However, in Ramakrishna there seems to be some
preference for the personal. That was the main
issue between him and the Brahmos that he encountered. He was always in communion with Divine
Mother. He said, "The term 'Mother' is very
sweet. Therefore, I like to call Him
'Mother'."46 In the same way Rámakrishna recog-

nized the value of any form of sincere approach to God. He used to refer to Hanumàna's attitude towards Ràma according to differences of his awareness of himself. When Hanumàn had <u>deha buddhi</u> body consciousness, he used to have the attitude of a servant towards his lord Ràma; when he had <u>jiva buddhi</u>, ego consciousness, he used to think himself as part of Ràma, and when he had <u>àtma buddhi</u>, awareness of his true being, he used to look upon Ràma as non-different from him. All these approaches are equally valid in so far they can lead humans in communion to the ultimate. However, Ràmakrishna seems to prefer the attitude of devotion. He said that body consciousness is almost inseparable from human consciousness. It is very difficult to get rid of the feeling of 'I' and 'mine.' As long as this feeling of 'I' and 'mine' remains the most effective spiritual path is to submit this 'I' to the Divine 'Thou' and thus devotion is the most effective spiritual path. Ràmakrishna was a non-dualist. He did not recognize the reality of anything else beyond or besides God. For him even the so called evils are also within God. Yet he did not emphasize <u>sa aham</u> ("I am that") but wanted to maintain the difference between 'I' and 'Thou.' He said "I do not want to become sugar but want to taste sugar."[47]

Panikkar's understanding of Hinduism can be justified from the perspective of Hinduism as presented in Ràmakrishna. It has to be kept in mind however that Ràmakrishna was opposed to any form of one-sidedness and exclusivity. He did not want to emphasize the personalistic or the non-personal aspect to the exclusion of each other. Ultimate reality is beyond any limit and hence can never be fully comprehended by limited humans. Pluralism therefore is acceptable without holding to absolute relativism. Panikkar thinks that this is one of the important contributions of Hinduism. He therefore tries to integrate his understanding of Hinduism with his understanding of Christianity and reformulate the Christian doctrines of Church, Christ, Trinity, etc. in his theological thinking. In the following chapter we shall try to explain his Christian theological thinking as it is developed in the course of his dialogue with Hinduism and investigate whether that is acceptable from the perspective of Catholicism.

Notes

Panikkar on Hinduism

[1] Panikkar, "Multi-Religious Experience,"
Anglican Theological Review, vol. 53, no. 4,
(Oct. 1971), p. 220.

[2] Id., The Trinity and Religious Experience
of Man (N.Y.: Orbis Books), p. xi.

[3] Id., Intra-Religious Dialogue (N.Y.:
Paulist Press, 1978), p.12.

[4] Ibid., p. 15.

[5] Panikkar wrote a few books comparing
Hinduism and Christianity. One such work as
Kultmysterium in Hinduismus und Christentum: Ein
Beitrag Zur Verleichenden Religions Theologie,
(Freiburg and Munchen, Karl Alber, 1964). A
French translation of this book Le Mystere du
Culte dan l'Hindouisme et le Christianisme was
published from Paris in 1970. Other works
include: Maya Apocalisse: L'incontro
dell'Induismo e del Christianeismo (Roma:
Abete, 1966), a Spanish translation of this book,
Misterio y Revelacion, was published from Madrid
in 1971; Kerygme und Indien: Zur
heilgeschichtliches Problematik der Christlichen
Begegnung mit Indien, (Hamburg: Reich Verlag,
1967). The Unknown Christ of Hinduism which was
Panikkar's Th.D. thesis was published from
London, (Darton: Longman and Tod) in 1964. This
is his most well-known work being written in
English. Besides the comparative works he has
written a few books exclusively on Hinduism. He,
with a number of helpers, produced the almost
1,000 page volume, The Vedic Experience:
Mantramanjari: An Anthology of the Veda for
Modern Man and Contemporary Celebration, (Los
Angeles and Berkeley: University of California
Press, 1977) and (London: Darton, Longman and
Tod, 1977). In the Spanish volumes of Compara-
tive Religions he contributed Algunos aspectos de
la espiritualidad hindu, La Espiritualidad
Comprada, vol. III, La Perfecion Cristoana, vida
Y Teori , eds. Baldomero Jimenes Duque and Luis
Sala Balust (Barcelona, Flors, 1969), pp.
433-542. In addition he has written more than
one hundred articles about Hinduism and
Christianity.

6 Hans Küng, On Being a Christian (N.Y.:
Doubleday, 1974), ch. 3.

7 A. Schweitzer's view is discussed by
Radhakrishnan in Eastern Religion and Western
Thought, Oxford: 1940.

8 Śamkara, Brahmasùtra Bhàsya, 1.1.3.

9 Panikkar, Trinity and the Religious
Experience of Man, p. 96.

10 Id., Los dioses y el Senor (Buenos
Aires: columba, 1967), p.97.

11 Id., The Vedic Experience:
Mantramanjari (California: University of California Press, 1977), p. 9.

12 Ibid., p. 653.

13 bid., p. 658.

14 Panikkar,   Trinity and Religious
Experience of Man. Also ''Towards an Ecumenical
Theandric Spiritualists," JES,   (Summer, 1968).
We shall discuss this point in the next chapter.

15 Panikkar, The Vedic Experience: p. 10.

16 Panikkar is not the only Catholic
theologian who is unhappy with the neo-Vedàntins.
The reason for this dislike is perhaps, as Sharpe
pointed out in Faith Meets Faith, the
neo-Vedàntins pose a challenge and a counter
apologetic to Christianity.

17 Panikkar, "Algunos Aspectos de la
Spiritualidad Hindu," La Spiritualidad Comprada,
vol. 3, La Perfecion Cristiana, Vida y Theoria,
eds. Baldomero Jimenes Doque and Luis Sala Blast,
(Barcelona: Flors, 1969), p. 433.

18 "El hinduismo..., no es una doctrina
(puede por tanto haber muchas doctrinas hindues)
ni una idea (no tiene entonce de coherencia
logica), ni una orgazacion, ni uno.   El hinduismo
no tiene limite alguno.   No tiene definicion.   So
cualquier cosa se probse ser "verdad," el
hinduismo es la aceptaria immediatmente como
propria.   El gran temor del hinduismo es que las
"verdades" (particles) desteuyan la Verdad

(total) in "Algunos Aspectos de la Spiritualidad Hindu," Ibid., pp. 436-437.

[19] "El hinduismo exige una conversion al orden factico de mera existencia para ser aprehendido." Ibid., p. 437.

[20] " Por la réspecto a la Verdad las admite todos en el ordenlógico." Ibid., p. 437.

[21] Poussen, The Way to Nirvana, Jaytileki refers to him in Early Buddhist Theories of Knowledge. London: Allen and Unwin, 1963.

[22] Panikkar, "Algunos Aspectos de la Spiritualidad Hindu," p. 437- 438.

[23] Ibid., p. 438.

[24] "Tiene que haber una continuidad: el samsàra, el ciclo de las existencias." Ibid., pp. 438-439.

[25] "Religion es el svadharma concretizado de una persona o de una grupo." Ibid., p. 439.

[26] "Lo que importa no es la 'idea,' el contenido, la formulacion de lo creido, sino el acto de creer." Ibid., p. 440.

[27] This is seen in Radhakrishnan, Indian Philosophy, vol. II, Chapter on Advaita Vedānta.

[28] Panikkar, "Algunos Aspectos," p. 112.

[29] "...mientras el Corán, para una concepción islámic ortodoxa contiene la Revelación de Dios a los hombres, mientras la Biblia narra los hechos y dichos más salientes del Revelador, directa (Nuevo Testamento) o indirectamente (Antiguo Testamento), la śruti es la misma Revelación." Ibid., p. 449.

[30] "Su consecucion exige entrega absoluta y consagracion, devecion total a este Bien. Solamente el amor puro y desinteresado conduce a El. El Bein no es tano un valor como una persona. He aqui el Bhaktimarga o el camino de la devoción. Su categoria fundamental es la persona y el amor su quintaesencia." Ibid., p. 465.

31 "Este sera el principio mismo de la
evolución y aun del abandono de la espiritualidad
kármica por los ostros dos caminos...: la
verdadera activitividad que hace al hombre, es el
conpeimiento, . . .; la accion real que nos hace
beber en la fuente misma del Ser y por tanto
participar de El y recibir su mismo Ser es la
devoción, el amor,...." Ibid., p.473.

32 R. C. Zeahner, Hinduism (London: Oxford
University Press, 1966; Reprint ed., 1971). Ch.
6.

33 Panikkar, "Algunos Aspectos," p. 471. ",La
incactividad no produce la liveración de la
acción por este mismo hecho, lleva a la
perfección. Ademas, no es ni siqiera
pisquicamente possible. Lo que occure es que la
acción tiene solamente valor cuando se realiza
como un sacrificio."

34 "Esta acció es una verdadera actividad
teándricale hombre ofrece sus actos a Dios, pero
es Dios quien los acepta y en fondo Dios quien
los realiza." Ibid., p. 472.

35 Panikkar, Le Mystere du Culte etc., p. 17.

36 Panikkar, "Algunos Aspectos," p. 472.

37 Ibid., p. 476.

38 Ibid., p. 477.

39 Ibid., footnote, p. 477.

40 Ibid., p. 478.

41 Sri Chaitany Charitāmrita-Aditilā.
Chapters 7, 39.

42 Ibid., Chapters 7, 5.

43 Ibid., Chapters 7, 73, 78, 83, 86, etc.

44 Nikhilananda, Gospel of Ramkrishna. P.
116.

45 Ibid., p. 132.

46 Ibid., p. 135.

47 Ibid., p. 147.

Chapter 3
Panikkar's Theological Thinking

Raimundo Panikkar is not a systematic theologian. All his theological thinking developed in the context of the plurality of world religions. Christianity proclaims that there is only one truth, one light, one way. Yet there is an enormous variety of traditions in the world. Panikkar starts his theological thinking from this existential situation. He himself mentions the dilemma1 of his situation. He was brought up in the strictest orthodoxy of Christianity; yet he is in a pluralistic milieu. Therefore, either he had to condemn everything around him as sin and error or he had to give up the exclusivistic and monopolistic notions that he was told embody truth. The different answers to his dilemma that are usually offered did not satisfy him. He says: "The eclectic answer flouts logic and sometimes common sense as well."[2] He could not accept the "orthodox" answer which, according to him, "merely concocts casuistic shifts,"[3] so that some nook is still left for those who profess error but not due to their own fault. It was difficult for him to live a life of orthodox Christianity with its exclusivistic claims, which seemed to him to be so unjust and false even if it were toned down with the notion of grace or election. He said that "the whole idea of belonging to a chosen people, of practicing the true religion, of being a privileged creature, struck me not as a grace but as disgrace."[4] He says that this is also unchristian and due to influences of Manichean, Puritan and Jansenistic thinking.[5]

However, he cannot give up his identity; he is a Christian, he lives by that faith. Therefore, he started to understand Christian exclusivism in an inclusivistic way. In the course of his dialogue with Hinduism (also Buddhism), Panikkar developed the idea of Christ as the unique and universal mediator between God and the world, thus not to exclude Iśvara or Tathāgata; the church as the mystical body of Christ which can be inclusive of the whole humanity; Christianity as the religion with the capital R which is the metanoia of all true religious tradition of the world. We can designate him as a theologian of dialogue.

Panikkar's theological thinking is not a deliberate intellectual attempt of interpretation of Christian exclusivism in an inclusivistic way. It is developed in the process of dialogue. And, dialogue according to Panikkar, itself is a religious act. Thus, his inter-religious dialogue is also an intra-religious dialogue. The tension produced by the contexts of different religions in his life produced tensions within his heart and, therefore, he went on with his internal monologue which is expressed in his theological thinking. In order to appreciate Panikkar, we have to keep this in mind. Again, true to the spirit of dialogue, we can also notice a growth and development in his theological thinking.

Panikkar's basic intuition regarding the relationships between Hinduism and Christianity and his understanding of Christianity, Christ, Trinity, Church, etc., seem to be the same in all his works. However, a growth and development in the sense of explicating the basic intuition in a more clear and distinctive way can be noticed in his later works. There is also some shift of emphasis in his later works. Though he always upholds the inseparability of the historical and transhistorical, in his later works, the emphasis shifts more to the transhistorical. This may be due to the growth and maturity of his thought. In his earlier works, his attitude seems to be like the first century Christians who were eagerly waiting for the imminent "parusia." In The Unknown Christ of Hinduism Panikkar says that if the Christian can properly deliver the message of Christianity, and the Hindu properly understands it, then the Hindu would welcome it.[6] In his later works, he has the maturer attitude of mutual fecundation, and thus growing together.

The Unknown Christ of Hinduism is Panikkar's first important work. It was his doctoral thesis for his Th.D., which he received from Roma in 1961. It was published in 1964 from London, and a reprint came out in 1968. And enlarged and revised second edition of the book is published from Bangalore, India. There are German, Spanish and French translations of this book. Its first preface is dated 1954. Die vielen Götter und der eine Herr was published from Weilheian in 1963 and was later translated into Spanish. Religione e Religioni was published from Brascia in 1964 and was translated into Spanish and German. All these works are pre-Vatican II. They present a bold attempt at making room for other traditions and not simply making room for the followers of other faiths. In other words, he does not simply want to speak of the "anonymous Christians," but calls the other traditions "proto Gospel."[7] He tries to indicate that the different traditions have some place in what the Christians consider the economy of salvation. In his effort to make room for other religions in the divine economy of salvation, Panikkar distinguishes between historical Christianity and Christianity, the historical and cosmic Christ, the Church as the vehicle of historical Christianity and as the community of humanity, and so on. He asserts that Christianity is more than historical Christianity, Christ is more than Jesus of Nazareth, yet he does not want to minimize in any way the importance of historical, not only for the professing Christians, but for the whole of humanity. In The Unknown Christ of Hinduism, he speaks of the "historical absoluteness of Christianity."[8] In Religionen und die Religion, though, he says that the claim of universality by any historical religion is only a historical claim, yet a few pages later, he says that Christianity, which has a definite historical beginning, is the most perfect religion.[9] In Los dioses y el señor, he says that Christianity as a faith in Christ is not one religion among others; it is the only religion. Christ is ever present--before Abraham. However, "He reveals himself at a specific time in history."[10] In these works, the thrust of the dialogue is still a passing of traffic from Christianity to other religions, bringing forth the hidden Christ of the different religions. In his later works like Trinity of the World Religions, published from Madras in 1970, and Salvation in Christ: Universality and Concreteness Supername, published from Santa Barbara in 1972, and also in his many articles of the 70s,[11] there is a shift more towards the universal--the cosmic aspect of Christ and Christianity than toward the particular historical. In Trinity and World Religions, he explicitly states that as a sociological religion, Christianity is only one among the many religions of the world and "is only one form among other possible ones of living and realizing the Christian faith."[12] In Salvation in Christ,

43

he warns against historicism and its result of
turning into idolatry. He points out that if, in
order to find the identity of Jesus, the emphasis
is placed on the spatio-temporal coordinates,
Christianity's claim of universality cannot be
justified. Not only that, "Indeed, if Christ
were only that, i.e., a reality merely of the
temporal and spatial order, which existed at a
certain time in history and had a certain place
in geography, the whole Christian faith would
collapse."[13] In his later works he still maintains that Christ is the fulfillment of all
religions. However, he says, "It is precisely
because I take seriously Christ's affirmation
that he is the way, the truth, and the life that
I cannot reduce his significance only to historical Christianity."[14] Panikkar not only takes
Jesus Christ's affirmation seriously, but he also
"take(s) seriously the sayings of the Gita that
all actions done with a good intention reaches
its goal, or the message of Buddha which points
out the way of liberation."[15] That is why at this
stage in dialogue with other religions his
emphasis is on mutual fecundation. The traffic
not only passes from Christianity to other
religions, but also from them to historical
Christianity. In The Trinity and World Religions, he uses Hindu notions of the different
ways of spirituality to understand the importance
of The Trinity. In particular he shows how
Advaita aids a deeper understanding of the
internal relationship of Trinity. Advaita also
helps to rescue Western Christianity from anthro-
pomorphism.

     For a systematic presentation of Panikkar's
theology, we must start with his notion of
religion. That would explain why he thinks
Christianity is the religion and also how his
view is influenced by Hindu Sanātana Dharma (The
Perennial Truth). Panikkar explicitly deals with
the question of what religion is in his work,
Religionen und die Religion. Here he tries to
discern the basic notion of religion in the
context of the plurality of religions. According
to him, where there is plurality and diversity,
the human mind naturally seeks a unity either in
a common denominator or in a unique and deep
identity, even if this unity expresses itself in
factual diversity. Humans cannot be content with
pluralism as the ultimate ground. "Even the mere
recognition of plurality includes a certain basic

unity, otherwise plurality would not even appear as diversity."[16]In this work, he gives a very broad definition of "religion" in order to indicate the unity of all religions. Religion is that virtue through which we worship and honor God and which is expressed in our ethical behavior. Virtue and practice are inseparable. Religions have the double aspect of doxa and praxis. It is that which leads humans to their goal or destiny. It enables them to transcend space and time while living in the world.

According to Panikkar, religion is concerned neither with divinity nor with humanity alone, but with the relationship between the two. Thus, all religions postulate (1) a reality beyond the human, (2) which is the end and goal of (3) humanity. Panikkar analyzes in great detail the anthropological basis of religion. Humanity, according to him, has nine dimensions. "Man is an always-becoming being, a pilgrim; man is (1st dimension), but more exactly, he is only in order to be on his way, he is not yet (8), he is a temporal being (9); his nature can be considered in relation to himself as an individual, or in relation to others as a social being. In the first case, he is intellect (2), will (3), and emotion or feeling (4); in the second he is social (5), telluric (6), and cosmic (7)." Corresponding to the nine dimensions of humanity, there are nine dimensions in religion, viz., (1) ontic-mystical, (2) dogmatic-doctrinal, (3) ethical-practical, (4) emotional, (5) ecclesiastical-sociological, (6) material-cosmological, (7) Angel-devil, (8) immanent-transcendent, (9) temporal-eternal.[17]

These dimensions indicate that religion has an inner and outer aspect, both of which are important. To leave out the inner aspect is to have a lifeless ritualism which does not lead to enlightenment. To leave out the outer aspect may lead to mere emotionalism which may degenerate into pure subjectivism. The philosophical analysis of religion does not deal with the diversity of the "contents" of different religions, the differences of the cultic performances, of the diversity of their actual existence. It shows the unity of the basic "structure" of all religions, as well as their "functional" unity. However, although the philosophical analysis cannot show any sign of visible

45

unity of all religions, it can support the
catholic faith which points toward that direction. The Greek word, kathalon, which is the
source of the word catholic, means to be on the
way--to lean toward universality, fullness,
perfection, totality, integrity and oneness.
Thus the exclusivity of Catholicism, like the
mathematical infinity, is inclusivistic; it is
universal. It is Religion with a capital R. It
is otologically the fullness of the nature of
religion. It fulfills the requirement of the
perfect religion as this is what leads humanity
to its ultimate destiny. This is Religion (i.e.,
Catholicism), whereas the different world traditions are only religions. According to Panikkar,
all religions ultimately lead to the true one
Catholic Religion. There may be many lights, but
one white beam. It takes many colors through
prism. Unless they all fall together again, they
are only partial. To the Christians, Christ is
the white beam which takes many colors through
the prism, and the Church is an inverted prism
that reconstitutes the fullness of human nature.
Catholic religion has no color; it is a white
beam. Catholic religion is more than historical
Christianity. It has a tendency of transdoctri-
nality, to infinity. "Christianity is not even a
religion, but it is the conversion of all religions."[18]

Panikkar on Christianity

        Panikkar wants to make a distinction between
Christianity as Religion par excellence and the
historical Christianity which is a major form in
which the super faith is lived. Historical
Christianity has its cultural associations and
limitations. Historical Christianity has a
definite beginning in time, with the birth of
Jesus of Nazareth, although the preparation for
it was going on from eternity. Not only is it
temporal as having a definite beginning in time,
it is also parochial, being originated and
developed in a certain area of space. The
semitic surroundings of its origin and its
development in the Mediterranean locations gave
Christianity its particular cultural coloring.
Historical Christianity is a particular religion
and cannot claim universality. "The claim of any
historical religion to be exclusive is only a
historical claim."[19] Like the other traditions of
the world, historical Christianity also needs to

46

be fulfilled in the Religion--the Christian
faith. Like other traditions of the world, it is
striving for the fulfillment.

Is historical Christianity, then, one among
the other traditions of the world? Is its
relationship with the super Religion the same as
that between the other religions and the super
Religion? In his earlier works, he explicitly
says that it is definitely not so. Historical
Christianity, though yet unfulfilled, is still
unique. The faith in Christ is concretely
expressed in historical Christianity. "Christianity is not just the action in the world, but
it is the concrete religion established by Christ
to be the normal and ordinary place of his
redeeming power and saving action."[20] It has the
fullness of divine revelation. It is the custo-
dian of the sacrament of Eucharist. Historical
Christianity, though fragmentary,

> has the consciousness of being a very spe-
> cially qualified 'fragment' indeed: the
> fulfillment of religion. This is not,
> however, because of her actual perfection,
> but because Christ, the Head of the Mystical
> Body is really and sacramentally present in
> her, and her soul is the Holy Spirit.[21]

Thus the relationship between Christianity and
historical Christianity and the relationship
between Christianity and other religions are not
on the same level. Historical Christianity is
not even the primer inter pares. Unlike the
other religions, it is itself a unique
religion.[22] The religions of the world are
related to Christianity not simply because it is
the Super-Religion, but also to historical
Christianity because

> Christianity is provisional and not
> self-sufficient--being only for this temporal
> existence and relying absolutely on Christ
> because there is no link from below, but only
> from above, but in such a way that the real
> transcendent call appears as an immanent
> urge.[23]

Thus, historical Christianity, although it does
not exhaust the Cosmic Christianity, is uniquely
significant for the whole of humanity as it is
the most concrete expression of the perfect

religion and is inseparable from it. In his
later works, although he admits the _sui generis_
relationship between Christianity as Super-Religion and historical Christianity, he is not
emphatic about the uniqueness of the historical
Christianity. In the _Trinity_ and _World_ _Reli-_
gions, he says that

> from the sociological and external point of
> view, Christianity is only one religion among
> others. One can therefore compare Chris-
> tianity with these other religions because it
> is one among the rest. From a sociological
> and even "scientific" point of view one
> cannot any longer consider Christianity as
> the whole of "religion" as if the rest were
> not "religions."[24]

However, there is a Catholic and Universal
religion which Panikkar still desires to call
Christianity, although he admits that others may
prefer to call it simply human, which "leads to
the plenitude and hence conversion of all religions, even though up to date it has only suc-
ceeded, from a Judaic substructure in converting
to a greater or lesser extent
helleno-latin-gothic-celtic 'paganism'."[25] This
Super-Religion is not something abstract; it is
not like Platonic essence; it gets "incarnated"
in historical forms, "but what we call Christianity is only one form among other possible
ones of living and realizing the Christian
faith."[26] His dialogue with other traditions made
it evident that to emphasize historical Christianity is not conducive to dialogue. He thinks
that there is neither practical nor theoretical
justification for such emphasis. However, he
wants to make it clear that as a matter of fact
the Super-Religion is incontestably lived in a
dominant way in the Western cultural form. But
to identify this sociological form with the
Christian faith itself is to "involve on the one
hand a 'particularism' incompatible with Catho-
licity and on the other an anachronistic theological 'colonialism' that is absolutely
unacceptable."[27]

Panikkar on Church

Like his distinction between
trans-historical and historical Christianity,
Panikkar makes a distinction between visible

Church and the Mystical Body. Of course, this
distinction is not made by Panikkar only. The
tension, created by the belief that the Church is
a concrete little flock, incarnated, historical
and historically committed to the facts of
history, and on the other hand, it is universal,
meant for the whole world, for everybody irres-
pective of the difference of race and cultures,
was present in Christianity since the time of
Paul. The release of this tension was attempted
in different ways. One such way is the idea of
the Church as the Mystical Body of Christ.
However, the problem of the relationship between
the visible Church and the Mystical Body remains.
Panikkar calls the visible Church sociological,
and the Mystical Body theological. The Church as
a social institution so far has been a product of
the Mediterranean world. Though it has been
claimed by this Church that it represents some
universal values which are valid for all humanity
as human, yet "There is no doubt that the church
in her doctrines, practices and even
self-understanding is by and large a product of
the mediterranean world."[28] Panikkar questions
whether it is possible in the context of the
present day world to have an unqualified condemnation of idol-worship, polygamy; or uphold the
views that bread and wine are indispensible for
the sacrament of Eucharist, or to think that only
certain philosophical systems are compatible with
Christianity. Panikkar says,

> Whereas some values may appear to be univer-
> sal for a certain degree of consciousness,
> they may look different from other angles of
> vision or for other forms of consciousness.
> On what grounds can one speak of (let alone
> impose) a universality de jure if there is no
> universality de facto.[29]

Some theologians uphold a minimalist view of
Church and consider it as the "remnant" of the
Lord with a very limited and particular mission.
They give up the claim of universality of Church
and believe that only the Reign would be universal. Others take a maximalist view and identify
Church with the congregation of the "Sons of Man"
as the people of God. For them it is difficult
to uphold the concreteness of Church. Panikkar
says that though the problem of the relationship
between sociological and theological Church is a
difficult question, yet the concepts are not

49

irreconcilable. It is possible to uphold concreteness and universality at the same time.

The fact that the church is visible does not
imply that its limits are visible to everybody or to anybody. Precisely because she is
visible, she presents the possibility of
different limits of visibility. Whereas some
do not see much beyond their churchyard,
others encompass a wider horizon. To affirm
then that Her confines touch the very limits
of mankind--without saying that they
coalesce--does not contradict the visibility
of the church.[30]

Panikkar's Christology

The same concern for concreteness and
universality is present in Panikkar's Christology. The Christians identify Christ with
Jesus the Son of Mary, yet claim that Christ is
the universal mediator; he is the universal
redeemer. Salvation is possible only in Christ.
The problem is: "If salvation is in Christ and
this salvation is offered to all men, how must we
understand this Christ, in whom alone there is
salvation?"[31]

Panikkar's understanding of Christ also goes
through a process of growth and development
though his basic intuition remains the same. In
the early works, he admits the importance of the
cosmic Christ. Yet he insists on the importance
of the historical Nazarene. In The Unknown
Christ of Hinduism, he says that Christianity and
Hinduism meet in "the ontic-intentional" stratum
which he calls Christ. But he mentions that a
full Christian faith further requires the identification of Christ with Jesus, the Son of Mary.
In the encounter with other religions, the cosmic
aspect of the Christ has to be emphasized.
Panikkar says that "the ultimate reason for the
universal idea of Christianity, an idea which
makes possible the Catholic embrace of every
people and religion...lies in the Christian
conception of Christ not only as the historical
redeemer, but also as the unique son of God, as
the second person of the Trinity, as the only
ontological--temporal and eternal--link between
God and the world."[32] However, one has to keep in
mind the specific character of Christianity:
"The historical and concrete dimension of Christ

50

which is yet 'inseparable' and 'indivisible' from
his divinity and his cosmic accion."[33] How can
the concrete and the universal be reconciled
remains a problem. In his later works, he
mentions the need for the development of a
universal Christology which is authentic and is
able to "make room for" different religions. He
makes such an attempt in <u>Salvation</u> <u>in</u> <u>Christ</u>:
<u>Concreteness</u> <u>and</u> <u>Universality</u> <u>the</u> <u>Supername</u>.
Here he attempts to develop a Christology
"keeping loyalty to the Christian tradition
without betraying other streams of mankind's
religious experience."[34]

According to Panikkar Christological understanding should emphasize the form rather than
the content, the personhood rather than the
individuality of Jesus Christ. In order to
answer the question, who is Jesus, if the
spatio-temporal coordinate is made the central
point of reference as is usually done by historically trained Western minds, it would make
Christian faith not only limited but also absurd.
It would make the Christian sacraments absurd; it
would make the scriptural saying that he is
yesterday, today and forever, he is before
Abraham,[35] etc., meaningless. The cosmic Christ
of the Epistles of Paul and the Gospel of John
would have no meaning.

No Christian will say that the living Jesus
of his faith is only a being of the past, not
affirm, on his other hand, that when, for
instance, he receives Christ in Eucharist, he
is eating the proteins of Jesus of Nazareth
who was walking in Palestine twenty centuries
ago.[36]

The traditional answer about who is Jesus as the
Messiah, he that cometh, the Son of Man or the
Son of God also are inadequate as they are
meaningful only under the Semitic context. These
are not meaningful for those who were not expecting any Messiah or who consider every person
to be Son of God. Here he refers to Hinduism.

Panikkar thinks that the clue to understanding who is Jesus is provided by Jesus
himself when he answered John the Baptist. Jesus
said, as is stated in Luke, 7:22-23,

Go and tell John what you hear and see: the
blind recover their sight, the lame walk, the
lepers are made clean, the deaf hear, the
dead are raised to life, the poor are bearing
the good news, and blessed is the man who
does not find me a stumbling block.

Here the emphasis is on function, not on substance or individuality of Jesus. Jesus' libe-
rating actions his mission, are important and not
his spatio-temporal individuality. Panikkar says
that the identity of the concrete and universal
Christ of the Christian faith, who is living, is
present in the sacraments and with whom one can
enter into an intimate, personal communion does
not fall under the category of singularity and
individuality. He is rather a person whose
characteristic is "not singleness, but communion,
not incommunicability, but relations."[37] Singularity is the category which is essentially related
to plurality-it refers to one among the many.
Obviously Jesus Christ cannot fall into this
category. Individuality implies difference from
the others, self-identity. Its reference is to
that which is distinctive. If we look for the
individuality of Jesus, we have to look for what
it is that makes Jesus, Jesus. Here the quest is
for a thing-in-itself, and not for the concrete,
living being. In the religious context, the
question is who is Jesus and not what is distinctive of Jesus. Or, in other words, it is the
inquiry about the person and not the individual.
The concept of person is relational. It involves
a network of relations between I-thou-she/he/it.
The notion of singularity and plurality is not
applicable to a person. Each person is unique.
The inquiry of the who of Jesus involves the
inquired and the inquirer both. Jesus as person
enters into the structure of our own personal
existence. Panikkar says that in Peter's answer
to Jesus as Thou art the Messiah, the Son of the
Living God,

the only universal element is thou and that
the fundamental issue is not so much to
elucidate intellectually the predicates of
the sentence, but to discover existentially
the subject, the real thou, who is more than
just a projection of my own ego. Now this
thou cannot be pinpointed by any unequivocal
means of identification and it is not without
reason that idolatry, i.e., the freezing of

the ineffable supreme in one particular
object of the senses or of the mind, is said
to be the greatest sin against the spirit.[38]

Jesus is the universal savior, not as an
individual, but as a person--in intimate relationship to those who are saved. Panikkar says
that,

Christ, the Saviour is, thus, not to be
restricted to the merely historical figure of
Jesus of Nazareth. Or, as we have already
said, the identity of Jesus is not to be
confused with historical identification.[39]

If Jesus were only a geographical and historical
reality, he would not be universal. He is
trans-historical though incarnated in history.
This understanding of Jesus makes it possible to
recognize "other saviours" who embody that saving
power which the Christians believe to be the
spirit of Jesus. Thus, Krsna can be a savior, as
can Buddha, as they are the expressions of the
cosmo-theandric principle.

In his understanding of Jesus, Panikkar does
not want to emphasize simply the incarnation or
the resurrection, but the Pentecost also. He
attempts to reconcile Western views with the
Eastern notions of Christ. This understanding is
conducive to ecumenism, the ecumenical ecumenism,
as this enables one to understand the universal
saving nature of Jesus Christ in the context of
the plurality of world traditions. The historical Jesus is historically connected to Semitic
religion. People of other faiths need not first
be converted to Semitism to be saved. Nor are
they saved by means of a general cosmic experience, which may be vague and abstract. They are,
rather, saved by means of their own concrete
human traditions.

Jesus in this case would be one of the names
of "the cosmo-theandric principle," which has
received practically as many names as there
are authentic forms of religiousness, and
which at the same time finds a historically
sui generis epiphany in Jesus of Nazareth.[40]

Panikkar thinks that an adequate theology of
religion which would be able to do justice to the
whole range of human religious experience would

be christocentric even if the Greek name Christ
is not mentioned, "for he does not stand only for
one single event, but for that 'cosmo-theandric
principle' which being incarnated in Jesus of
Nazareth, has not only spoken many times through
the prophets, but has not also left himself
without witnesses in any moment of history."[41]
The Hindu notion of Avatāra and the Buddhist's
notion of Tathāgata has the same function.

Jesus Christ is the only true mediator.
Being cosmo-theandric, He is the center of the
cosmic mandala from which the whole of reality
emerges and into which it goes. Everything that
is comes from and is referred to this center.
Everything is Christophany.[42] Proper understanding of Jesus Christ implies its Trinitarian
context.

Panikkar's Understanding of Trinity

According to Panikkar, the Trinitarian
understanding of God-head and the Cosmo-theandric
vision of reality is an absolute necessity, not
only for a theoretical understanding of the
problem of transcendence and immanence, but also
for the practical needs of a more just society or
more integral human personality.[43] It shows the
interrelatedness of all values as they are based
on an interrelated reality. Panikkar mentions
theandrism in most of his later works. What
exactly he means by theandric intuition of
reality he states very clearly in one of his
presentations in the Monchanin Centre of Montreal
in 1975. He says,

> The cosmo-theandric intuition would be that
> vision which, I repeat, brings together every
> scientific thread as well as all the other
> manifestations of the human spirit and
> discovers, to put it simply, that:
>
> > There is no God without Man and the
> > World
> > There is no Man without God and the
> > World
> > There is no World without God and Man.[44]

Then he goes on to explain the three terms which
he calls symbols. By God he understands that
dimension which is without dimension. It is plus

54

ultra, i.e., infinite, that direction of which no
human is master. It is the mysterious dimension
of anything real. By human being he means
anthropos as distinct from God. By world he
means the cosmos, the entire physical reality.
These three, though distinct, are integrally
related with each other and are what they are
because of this relationship. To object that
there could be a God without the creation is not
any objection as this itself is affirming that it
is not so. Panikkar says that "we can, we even
must, distinguish and discriminate, but we cannot
close communication between spheres of the
real."[45] This cosmo-theandric vision is one of
the deepest of human intuitions. It is "the
intuition of the three-fold structure of reality,
the triadic oneness existing on all levels of
consciousness and of reality, of the Trinity."[46]
Trinity, according to Panikkar, is that acme of
truth which permeates all reality of being and
consciousness.

Thus, according to Panikkar, the doctrine of
Trinity is not simply to satisfy the curiosity
about the "immanent" Trinity as an internal
affair of the Divinity (ad intra) alone. It
shows the connection between the immanent Trinity
and the "economic" God (ad extra) in which the
destiny of the whole world lies. The doctrine of
the Trinity "is not mere speculation about the
depths of God; it is equally an analysis of the
heights of man."[47]

Trinity is the reconciliation of the
opposites--matter and spirit, humanity and God,
traditional God and no-God. It makes it impossible to consider God as totally "other." Such a
God can have no relationship to humanity.
Similarity, it makes it impossible to view
humanity in separation from God.

The Trinity, in fact, reveals that there is
life in the God-head as well as in Man, that
God is not an idol, nor a mere idea, nor an
ideal goal of human consciousness. Yet he is
neither another substance nor a separate, and
thus separable reality.[48]

Trinity is the basis for true ecumenism as
only Trinity can do justice to the different
forms of spirituality that are present in the
different world traditions without emphasizing

anyone of them to the exclusion of the others. Panikkar distinguishes three basic types of spirituality. First is iconolatry, which is purer form of "idolatry" insofar as it specifies God and makes God into an object, though aware of the fact that God cannot be so specified and objectified. This form of spirituality is present even in the pure monotheism of Judaism which abhors any form of idolatry. The Jewish idea of God who makes a pact with humanity and can be appeased, is iconolatric. The second form of spirituality is personalism. Instead of an icon, the religious symbol here is a person. Christianity is particularly emphatic in depicting God as a person. This trend of spirituality sometimes tends to be purely anthropomorphic. The third form of spirituality is represented by the idea of supra-personal Absolute. It recognizes a spirit that inspires rather than enters into dialogue with humanity. This type of spirituality is present in some Upanishads. The Absolute is then found in the realm of transcendence. This type of spirituality emphasizes only the Absolute and disregards the human aspect of religion.

Panikkar thinks that Trinity can reconcile and synthesize these basic forms of spirituality. The Father corresponds to the Absolute--it is the apophatic--the transcendent aspect of God-head. Nothing can be said of the Father. He is nothing except that through generating the Son and the Spirit he has given everything. Non-being is the source of Being. Son is the Being of the Father; in him everything exists. He is the personal aspect of the God-head with whom humanity can enter into relationship. Son need not be identified with Jesus of Nazareth. "Every being is a Christophany, fully divine and human, if he participates in the son."[49] The Spirit is the immanent aspect of the God-head--it is the ground of Being and beings. It is the communication between the Father and the Son and completes the circle.

Thus, the Trinity may be summarized as Father--Source, Son--Being, Spirit--Return of Being. The term Theandric is preferable to the term Trinitarian because it synthesizes better the three basic dimensions of life.[50]

Consequences of Panikkar's Christological Thinking

Certain consequences regarding dialogue between Christianity and other traditions follow from Panikkar's theological thinking. Dialogue is not between the Super-Religion Christianity and the other traditions, but between the different historical expressions of the one true religion, all of which, of course, are not equally true. It encourages the principle of relativity, but not relativism. All the traditions are interrelated insofar as they are leading toward their conversion in the Religion. Mutual influence-mutual fecundation can be conducive to this conversion. As Hinduism can profit from its contact with Christianity, historical Christianity also can learn from Hinduism.

Panikkar calls this inter-religious dialogue also as intra-religious dialogue insofar as it is accompanied by the monologue of the believer. However, from Panikkar's perspective, inter-religious dialogue can be called intra-religious for another reason. According to Panikkar's theological thinking, nothing can be outside Christianity. Christ is the second person of the cosmo-theandric principle. He is the ontological mediator between God and creation, "the whole created existence being nothing else than a Christophany."[51] Thus, nothing can be outside Christ and, in this sense, there cannot be any non-Christians and non-Christian religion. Therefore, dialogue is always intra-religious.

Panikkar thinks that to call any religion non-Christian would mean that there are religions outside the Christian economy and thereby would reduce the universal claim of Christianity to a false claim. It "will reduce 'Christianity' to a mere sect and Christian faith to being one among many."[52]

Christianity as a historical religion cannot claim exclusivity regarding truth, knowledge of the truth or salvation. Its teachings are not unique. Similarity of ethical precepts of different religions can be easily recognized. The moral law regarding one's relationship to his neighbor as presented in the Code of Manu does not seem to be different from "turning the other cheek." Manu said: "Do not hurt your neighbor, even if he provokes you: do not harm any body by thought or action, do not prefer words which may be painful to others" (Laws of Manu, II:161). He quotes from other precepts of Manu to disprove the uniqueness of Christianity. Panikkar thinks that the similarities of teachings rather show how Christ is working in the different religions.[53]

Panikkar's cosmo-theandrism promotes the idea of universal love. The Christians, because of their faith in their relationship to God, have to accept the same relationship with the world. The world cannot exist independently of God and apart from God. Creation is ex nihilo, but also, "a Deo, and in Deo, from God and in God. ...so the Christian by one and the same act by which he 'reaches' God also 'embraces' his world."[54]

Hindu Elements in Panikkar's Theological Thinking

Panikkar's idea that religion is the way of leading humans to their destiny is in agreement with Hinduism. His idea that Christianity is the Super Religion also can be considered as a result of Hindu influence. It is similar to the idea of Sanātana Dharma. The Hindu idea is that there is only one truth and that truth is expressed variously in diverse forms of religion. Panikkar is appreciative of the Hindu attitude of unity with diversity. He considers that this attitude can be of help for interpretation of the Gospels. He says: "Many a present day interpretation of the Gospels could win insight and avoid unnecessary problems if only envisaged under the perspective offered by India even today."[55]

The Hindu idea as is expressed by Rāmakrishna that all religions are equal is often ridiculed without understanding its true import. It does not state that all religions are the same or profess the same beliefs. It means that all religions insofar as they can lead humans to their goal are true, and hence in that respect equal. Panikkar's functional view of religion is in agreement with Hinduism as taught by Rāmakrishna.

However, there is a difference between Panikkar and Vedāntic ideas of religion. Speci-

58

fically, advaida Vedānta in agreement with
Buddhism considers religion useful for attaining
moksa (salvation). However, it has no final
validity. Rather if it is held on to, it becomes
a hindrance. Following the aurvedic (medicinal)
analogy, Buddha said that his religious teachings
are like medicine to cure disease of worldly
defilement. After curing the disease, if the
medicine is not dissolved in the process and
remains as a remnant, then this itself becomes a
cause of defilement.

Again, according to this view, in general no
religion can be perfect insofar as they are human
ways of looking at the ultimate. In this respect, the Hindu view is somewhat similar to Karl
Barth, although like Karl Barth, Hindus do not
consider religion as human vanity. Panikkar not
only believes in the possibility of ultimately
true religion, for him to be ultimately true is
characteristic of any true religion. All the
traditions of the world, insofar as they are
progressing toward being ultimately true are true
religion. He calls the ultimately true religion
Christianity, although he does not deny that
others may prefer to call it by some other name.
All the world traditions, by being ultimately
true, would not merge in an abstract universal
truth, but they would still be the concrete
specific religions. Panikkar's concern is
universality together with concreteness. Reconciliation of these two has been a philosophical
problem--both for East and West.[56] Panikkar wants
to make a distinction between Hinduism and
Christianity by stating that, whereas, "Hinduism
is the religion of truth, Christianity is true
religion."[57] That is, Hinduism is abstract, but
Christianity is universal and concrete. Hinduism, due to functional equivalence of all traditions, does not ascribe any special status to any
particular religion. Although Panikkar admits
this functional similarity of all religions and
recognizes the limitations and short-comings in
all historical forms of religion, yet to him
historical Western Christianity has a special
status. He follows Hinduism in his de-emphasis
of history. Yet he says that Christianity is
both historical and trans-historical. The
SuperReligion is more manifestly incarnated in
the historical forms of Western Christianity than
anywhere else. Christ is manifest in historical
Christianity--only hidden in Hinduism. So there

59

seems to be a hierarchy here for which he criticizes the neo-vedāntins.

The influence of Hinduism is more evident in
Panikkar's understanding of the Trinity or
theandrism. Although the interrelatedness of the
three may be considered a result of Buddhist
influence, the Hindu idea of advaita,
non-duality, helped him to understand how the
three persons of the Trinity can be one, yet
three. Trinity or theandrism can give an integral view of reality. Hinduism teaches three ways
of spirituality. An integral pursuit of all
these three would correspond to theandrism. In
this respect, Panikkar's view is very similar to
Sri Ansobhindo's integral yoga. In the next
chapter we shall discuss Hindu views of Christ.
It would show how Panikkar must have been influenced by Radhakrishnan. At least they are
addressing themselves to the same kind of problems.

In Christianity, Logos Christology is recognized to be a universalizing element. Pannikar
indicates that too much emphasis on logos can
ultimately lead to anthropomorphic religion. It
is evident in Western forms of Christianity.
Panikkar thinks that Hindu advaita can rescue
Western Christianity from this anthropomorphic
tendency. Advaita represents the Holy Spirit of
the Trinity. In this respect, his view is
simdlar to Monchanin. Advaita is not pantheism
or monism. It emphasizes the immanent aspect of
the God-head. It therefore also indicates the
nonpersonalistic aspect of the God-head.

Panikkar and Christianity

Hindu influence on Panikkar may make him
suspect from the perspective of Christianity.
Some of his Christian critics are unhappy[58] about
his de-emphasis of the historical Jesus. It is
difficult to appreciate Panikkar from the perspective of Western Christianity whose forerunner
is Augustine. In Augustine the emphasis is on
unity of God, and not on Trinity. Panikkar
emphasizes Trinity. Karl Rahner in contemporary
Catholic theology emphasizes the importance of
Trinity in Christian theological thinking.
Panikkar thinks that his view is not outside
tradition. The theologies of early Greek fathers
as well as Bonaventure can justify his view. If

we note the early fathers like Justin, Ireneous
or Clement of Alexandria, it seems Panikkar's
claim is justified. All of them advocated a
trinitarian doctrine of creation and hence no one
can be left out from the province of salvation.
The cosmic vision of Christ is present in all of
them. We can easily notice Justin's emphasis on
Christos--the cosmic Christ than the Jesus of
Nazareth when he says:

> The Son of God, who alone is properly called
> Son, the Word which was with him and was
> begotten before all things, when in the
> beginning he (God the Father) created and
> arranged (ekosnise) all things through him,
> is called Christ, because he was annointed
> and because God the Father arranges all
> things of creation through him.[59]

Ireneaus, who is considered as the founder
of the theology of history, also emphasizes the
cosmic Christ. Revelatory history is coequal
with the history of the world. Christ always
reveals his faith as the Father is revealed
through the son.

> This form revelaverit does not refer only to
> future--as if the Word had only then begun to
> manifest the Father, when he was born from
> Mary--but it refers to all times. For, from
> the beginning is the Son with his creatures
> and reveals the Father to all those the
> Father wills, and when he wills and how he
> wills. And for this reason there is in all
> things and through all things one God, the
> Father, and one Word, and one Son, and one
> Spirit, and one Salvation for those who
> believe in him.[60]

In Clement of Alexandria also we see the
emphasis on the cosmic--on Logos--and not simply
on historical Jesus. Logos is present in all
humanity. That is why, by virtue of human reason
also, humanity can have some idea of God. Logos
is ever present in the world. Thus there had
always been prophets as well as philosophers who
did speak of God. Clement not only mentioned the
presence of Logos in Jewish law and the Hellenic
philosophers, he also mentioned its presence
among the Hindus and the Buddhists. "The Indian
gymnosophists and other non-Greek philosophers,
of whom there are two classes, the Sarmanac and

the Brahmanas.... Some, too, of the Indians obey
the precepts of Buddha."[61]

Panikkar's emphasis on spirit--the immanent
aspect of the Godhead-can have its parallel in
Bonaventure. Bonaventure, in _Itinerarium Mentis
in Deum_, shows how the universe manifests the
power, wisdom and goodness of the Triune God. He
considers the physical universe a mirror reflecting the glory of God.[62] E. Cousins, in
"Trinity and World Religion,"[63] pointed out how
Panikkar's view regarding the relationship of
Christianity and the other traditions based on a
Trinitarian understanding can be justified from
within the tradition.

That Panikkar is within the Christian
traditions can be verified by comparing his
theological thinking with Karl Rahner, who is the
recognized orthodox Catholic theologian of
contemporary Catholicism. The term "anonymous
Christians" introduced by Karl Rahner fell into
ill repute both in missionary circles as well as
among non-Christians. The real intention of
Rahner in such a designation seems to be to
emphasize the fact that Christ is the universal
mediator in the sense that through and in him
every thing is created. Hence there cannot be
any one who is outside the Christian realm and
possibility of salvation. It is the Logos which
is incarnated in Jesus of Nazareth. Thus it can
be said, as Panikkar does, that Christ is more
than historical Jesus. The difference between
Rahner and Panikkar seems to be about the relationship of Jesus to the Logos and in that
context the relationship between Jesus and the
other saviors in other religious traditions.
Panikkar believes that in Jesus there is the
fullest manifestation of the Logos. Yet it is
possible that it is manifested in others as well.
He is not as emphatic about the qualitative
difference between Jesus and the other saviors.
He is hesitant to equate Jesus and Krsna, but
willing to recognize their functional equivalence.[64] Rahner in his idea of "anonymous Christians" does not deny the possibility of salvation
of the non-Christians by their own traditions.
Hence by implication he cannot deny other saviors. However in him there seems to be an
emphasis on the once and for allness of the
nature of incarnation in Jesus. He offers an
evolutionary Christology. Jesus is Savior as

historical subjectivity--the preparation of which
started from the beginning of creation and is
expressed in human subjectivity. Yet Jesus is
the one unique universal savior. Rahner says,

> We are calling saviour here that histo-
> rical subjectivity in which, first, this
> process of God's absolute self-communication
> to a spiritual world as a whole exists irre-
> vocably; secondly, that process in which this
> divine self-communication in which God's
> self-communication reaches its climax insofar
> as this climax must be understood as a moment
> within the total history of human race, and
> as such must not simply be identified with
> the totality of spiritual world under God's
> self-communication.[65]

Rahner thinks that insofar as self-communication
is free, both on the part of God and the history
of human race, it is perfectly legitimate to
employ the notion of an event through which this
self-communication and acceptance reaches a point
in history which is irrevocable and
irreversible.[66]

Similarity of Panikkar and Rahner is very
evident in their emphasis on as well as in their
understanding of the Trinity. According to
Panikkar the Trinity is the best expression of
spirituality, being the most integral. Rahner
thinks that the Trinity of Christianity distinguishes it from monolithic monotheism. He is
unhappy of the average Western Christian's
unawareness of Trinity.[67] Rahner thinks that the
possibility of creation and redemption is
grounded in the Trinity. The "immanent Trinity"
is the "economic Trinity" and vice versa. Like
Panikkar Rahner believes that Trinity can be
better understood in terms of their mutual
relationship than in terms of their substantive
unity. Like Panikkar Rahner also thinks that the
Christian idea of the God-head is better expressed by the early Greek Fathers than the Latin
Church. He thinks that the emphasis on the unity
of God can be traced back to Augustine who, by
starting with the unity of God's essence and then
discussing the three persons, separated the
treatises On One God and On The Triune God.
Since Augustine's time this is the procedure of
padegogy. Rahner thinks that the Trinity represents the unorginated God, the Father, as well as

His self-communication through "Son" and "Spirit"
Son as the revelation of the Father to the human
beings and spirit as grace in human response to
this revelation.[68] panikkar's idea of Father as
the non-Being the apophatic source of everything,
Son as Being and Spirit as return of Being is
quite similar in Spirit. Although all the
Catholics do not and would not agree with
Panikkar entirely yet Panikkar's view can be
recognized to be Catholic.

Notes

Panikkar's Theological Thinking

1 Panikkar, Intra-Religious Dialogue (N.Y.:
Paulist Press, 1978), chap. 1.

2 Ibid., p. 5.

3 Ibid., p. 5.

4 Ibid., P. 6.

5 Panikkar, "Christians and the So-called
Non-Christians," Cross Current, Vol. 22, No. 3
(Summer-Fall, 1972), p. 285.

6 Id., The Unknown Christ of Hinduism
(London: Darton, Longman á Todd, 1964).

7 Ibid., p. 39.

8 Ibid., p. 45

9 Panikkar, Religionen Und die Religion,
(Munchen: Max Hueber, 1965), p. 160.

10 Id., Los dioses y el Senor (Buenos Aires:
Columba, 1967), p. 13.

11 Some of Panikkar's articles of 1970s
include: "The Category of Growth in Comparative
Religion: A Critical Self-Examination," The
Harvard Theological Review, Vol. 66, No. 1 (Jan.,
1973); "Christians and the So-Called
Non-Christians," Cross Current, Vol. XXII, No. 3
(Summer Fall, 1972), etc.

12 Panikkar, The Trinity and the Religious
Experience of Man (New York: Orbis Books and
London: Darton, Longmar á Todd, 1973), p. 4.

13 Id., Salvation in Christ (published
privately from Santa Barbara, 1972), p. 23.

14 Id., "The Category of Growth in Compara-
tive Religion: A Critical Self Examination,"
Harvard Theological Review, Vol. 66, No. 1
(January, 1973), p. 113.

15 Ibid., p. 113.

16 Panikkar, _Religionen und die Religion_. p. 13.

17 Referred to by Peter Schriener, "The Attitu of Catholic Theology to Non-Christian Religion," a Thesis. Department of Religion, October, 1966, pp. 77-78.

18 Panikkar, _Los dioses y el Senor_, p. 104.

19 Id., _Religionen und die Religion_, p. 158.

20 Id., _The Unknown Christ of Hinduism_. p. 34.

21 Ibid., p. 22.

22 Ibid., p. ix.

23 Ibid., p. 63.

24 Panikkar, _The Trinity and Religious Experience of Man_, p. 4.

25 Ibid., p. 4.

26 Ibid., p. 4.

27 Ibid., p. 4.

28 Panikkar, _Salvation in Christ_, p. 9.

29 Ibid., p. 10.

30 Ibid., p. 15.

31 Ibid., p. 10.

32 Panikkar, _The Unknown Christ of Hinduism_, p. 57.

33 Ibid., p. 17.

34 Panikkar, _Salvation in Christ_, p. 18.

35 Hebrews XIII:8 and VIII:58.

36 Panikkar, _Salvation in Christ_, p. 23.

37 Ibid., p. 32.

38 Ibid., pp. 40-41.

[39] Ibid., p. 51.

[40] Ibid., pp. 71ff.

[41] Ibid., p. 72.

[42] In The Unknown Christ of Hinduism. Panikkar shows the similarity of function of Christ and Iśvara. We shall refer to it in some detail in Chapter 5 of our thesis.

[43] Panikkar, The Trinity and Religious Experience of Man, p. xii.

[44] Panikkar, "Echology," Monchanin. vol. 7, nos. 3-5 (June December, 1975), p. 27.

[45] Ibid., p. 27.

[46] Panikkar, The Trinity and Religious Experience of Man, p. xi.

[47] Ibid., pp. xii ff.

[48] Ibid., p. xiii.

[49] Panikkar "Towards an Ecumenical Theandric Spirituality," Journal of Ecumenical Studies,(Summer, 1968), p. 508.

[50] Ibid., p. 508.

[51] Panikkar, "Christians and the So-called Non-Christians," p. 285.

[52] Panikkar, "Church and the World Religions," Religion and Society; Bangalore, vol. 14, no. 2, 1967. P. 60.

[53] Quoted in Panikkar, "The Relationship of Gospel to Hindu Religion and Culture," in Jesus and Man's Hope, Vol. 2, p. 250.

[54] Panikkar, "Christians and the So-Called Non-Christians," p. 285.

[55] Panikkar, "The Relationship of Gospel to Hindu Culture and Religion," p. 253.

[56] This is evident in Nyāya discussion of the relationship of universal and particular and

the discussion of universal and particular in Plato and Aristotle.

57 "El hinduismo pretende ser la Religión de la Vedad. El Cristianismo cree ser la Vedad de la Religion." (Panikkar, "Algunos Aspectos," p. 441.)

58 One example is Nalini Devadas, "The Theandrism of Panikkar and Trinitarian Parallels in Modern Hindu Thought," J.E.S., forthcoming.

59 Justin (a. Apol., 6, 3), quoted in James Dupuis, Jesus Christ and His Spirit (Bangalore: Theological Publications in India, 1977), p. 6.

60 Irenaeus, (Adv. Haer., IV, 6, 7) quoted in Dupuis, p. 11.

61 Clement of Alexandria (Strom, 1, 15), quoted in Dupuis, p. 17.

62 E. Cousins, "Trinity and World Religions," Journal of Ecumenical Studies (Summer, 1970), p. 484.

63 Ibid., p. 476-498.

64 Panikkar, Intra-Religious Dialogue, p. 15.

65 K. Rahner, Foundations of Christian Faith (New York: Seabury Press, 1978), p. 199.

66 Ibid., p. 196.

67 Rahner, The Trinity, Tr. J. Doncel. N.Y.: Harder and Harder, 1970. P. 10 ff.

68 Ibid., chap. 3.

Part II

Vedāntic Investigation of Panikkar

Chapter 4

Panikkar and Some Hindu Views About Christ and
Christianity

In the first part of our discussion we
presented Panikkar's understanding of Hinduism
and its Hindu authenticity, and the integration
of this understanding to his theological thinking
and its Catholic authenticity. According to
Panikkar's proposed scheme of dialogue this is
adequate. However, he maintains the ideal
situation exists when the integrated spiritual
thinking is acceptable to both the partners of
the dialogue. We did not come across any Hindu
written response to Panikkar. Discussion with
Hindu thinkers and religionists brought out
negative responses. They believe that Panikkar
is using Hindu premises to prove a Christian
conclusion. Among the Hindus a general reluctance to be involved in dialogue with the Christians can be noticed. Most Hindus are condi-
tioned by the history of the encounter with
Christianity. Contact and conversation between
the Christians and the Hindus were not on terms
of equality. Christians tried to teach the Truth
to the Hindus--they tried to proselytize. Most
Hindus think the proposal of dialogue is another
trick on the part of Christians to convert them.
Our analysis of Panikkar's view of dialogue
indicated that dialogue is not for teaching the
truth to the partner of dialogue but to investigate about it together. In the process any one
or both the partners may have to give up his or
her prior ideas and understandings. A person
involved in dialogue faces the risk of being
converted. But he or she has the opportunity of
being enriched by some deeper understanding of
what he or she considered as Truth before.
Hinduism may not have any universal dogma, but
most of the modern Hindus are proud about Hindu
tolerance, its universalistic view of Truth. To
be true to this spirit of universalism the Hindus
have to take dialogue between the religions
seriously. Our proposed Vedāntic investigation
of Panikkar, although itself is not a dialogue,
insofar as it can show the possibility of any
positive response towards the spiritual vision of

69

Panikkar, can be a contribution in the field of Hindu-Catholic dialogue. It would demonstrate the possibilities as well as the problems of this kind of dialogue.

Our Vedāntic investigation of Panikkar would be in two chapters. First we shall present the thinking about Christ and Christianity by some nineteenth and twentieth century Hindu thinkers all of whom are Vedāntins in one way of another. These thinkers were pre-Panikkar. Panikkar in his theological thinking addressed himself to some of the issues raised by these thinkers. A comparison of these thinkers and Panikkar can demonstrate to what extent Panikkar's thinking is acceptable from their perspectives. These modern Hindu thinkers may be grouped under the two classical schools of Vedānta-advaita and viśistādvaita. In the following chapter by way of a comparison of these two schools of Vedānta with Panikkar's cosmo-theandric view of spirituality we shall attempt to see how far it is possible to respond positively to Panikkar from the perspectives of these schools of Vedānta.

Panikkar said that other than Christians, only Hindus had detailed and various Christiological thinking.[1] This however is a recent phenomenon in the history of the encounter of Hinduism and Christianity. The history of the contact of India and Christianity is quite ancient. Even if the claim of the Thomas Christians of south India that their Church was established by the apostle may not be conclusively demonstrated historically, there is nonetheless sufficient historical evidence to indicate that Christianity was present in India in very early Christian centuries.[2] However, Christianity did not make any impact on Hindu thinking until nineteenth century. In the early period of the encounter Christianity was confined mainly to the low caste Hindus who were in the fringe of Hindu society. After eighteenth century British conquest of India the missionary and evangelical movements became quite powerful and stimulated Hindu responses to Christ and Christianity. The responses were typically Hindu. It was not denial of one and acceptance of the other but an absorption of the new, and a growth and revitalization of the old. One reason for the limited number of Christian converts among the Hindus is the nature of Hinduism itself. Hinduism accepts

within its fold varieties of faiths. Hindus
could incorporate what they understood about
Christianity into their own faith. Thus, some
Hindus accepted Jesus as their Iṣṭadevatā.[3] The
Hindu religious leaders wrote admiringly about
Jesus and his teachings, but did not find in the
Gospel teachings anything dramatically different
from Hinduism. For them it is the return of the
perennial. They identified the exclusivistic
interpretation of the Gospel by the Christian
missionaries, with the Churchianity of the West.

This appreciation of Jesus and condemnation
of institutional Christianity is prominent in all
of the writings of the nineteenth and twentieth
century Hindu writers. Keshab Sen, the most
prominent Brahmo leader after Rammohan Roy, wrote
how deeply he was influenced by Christ. "My
Christ, My Sweet Christ, the brightest jewel of
my heart, the necklace of my soul--for twenty
years I have cherished him in my miserable
heart.... The mighty artillery of his love he
levelled against me, and I was vanquished and
fell at his feet, saying--Blessed child of God,
when shall others see the light that is in
thee?"[4] The passion in these lines can be compared to the passion of Augustine and Luther.
However, he insisted that Christ is not Christianity and he refused to accept institutional
Christianity. He said: "I repudiate the little
Christ of popular theology, and stand up for a
greater Christ, a fuller Christ, a more eternal
Christ."[5] He envisioned a unity of all religions
in his universalized understanding of Christ.
"Surely the future Church in this country will be
the result of purer elements of the leading
creeds of the day, harmonized, developed and
shaped under the influence of Christianity."[6]

Swami Vivekānanda writes about Christianity
more in polemical terms than Kesab Sen and tries
to prove the superiority of Vedāntic Hinduism to
Christianity as a basis of any universal religion. He said:

Just as our God is an Impersonal yet a
Personal God, so is our religion a most
intensely impersonal one, and yet it has an
infinite scope for the play of persons, for
what religion gives you more incarnations,
more prophets and seers, and still waits for
infinitely more?... It is in vain we try to

71

gather all the peoples of the world around a single personality. It is difficult to make them gather together even around eternal and universal principles.[7]

Vivekānanda indicated the problem of universalization of Christianity when it absolutised one spatio-temporal event (Jesus of Nazareth) to be ultimate. However, Vivekānanda took his monastic vows along with nine other disciples of Rāmkrishna on a Christmas Eve. Before the ceremony he recounted the story of Jesus' life to his fellow brothers and urged them to be Christs by imitating Christ. They pledged themselves to work for the redemption of the world, and deny themselves as Jesus has done.[8] Even now Christmas is celebrated in the 'Rāmakrishna math' in Belur near Calcutta every year. The motto of Rāmakrishna order, "Ātmanam moksārtha Jagat hitayaca" (ones own salvation and well being of the world) is analogous to the Christian ideal "love God with all thy heart and love thy neighbor as thyself."

Gandhi, the father of Indian nation, advocated worship of Truth rather than worship of any personality as religion. Worship of personality may amount to idolatry. Christians may worship Jesus of Nazareth as long as they "only remember that truth is not one of the many qualities that we name. It is the living embodiment of God, it is the only life, and I identify Truth with the fullest life, and that is how it becomes a concrete thing. God is His whole creation, the whole existence, and service of all that exists--truth--is service of God."[9] Gandhi, however, explicitly states that the example of Jesus' suffering underlies his faith in the nonviolence. He says: "Though I can not claim to be a Christian in the sectarian sense, the example of Jesus' suffering is a factor in the composition of my underlying faith in non-violence, which rules all my actions worldly and temporal. Jesus lived and died in vain, if he did not teach us to regulate the whole life by the eternal law of love."[10] One of the formative forces for Gandhi was the Bhāgavad Gitā. He memorized all its verses and constantly referred to it to resolve his doubts and conflicts. Gandhi equated the teachings of the Sermon on the Mount with the teachings of Bhāgavad Gitā. He said, "Today supposing I was deprived of the Gitā and forgot all its contents but had a copy of the Sermon, I should derive the same joy from it as I do from the Gitâ."[11]

The impact of Christianity on contemporary Hinduism is unquestionable. The above examples come from the three chief movements within modern Hinduism. Kesab Sen represents the Brahmo Samaj movement, which was primarily a social reform movement. Vivekânanda represents the revival of Vedântic Hinduism, which is one of the most important attempts at systematizing Hinduism in modern times. Gandhi represents the nationalist movement of Hinduism. These different movements are not exclusive of each other, though differences of emphasis can be distinguished. All of them openly admired the teachings of Jesus. From the history of the encounter between Christianity and Hinduism, it seems that any Hindu who came in contact with the teachings of the Gospel, as they understand it, responded positively to it. However, all along there seems to be a resistance to the missionary attempts at conversion. The causes for this resistance are complex. The feeling of national pride, the foreignness of the ecclesiastic form of religion to the Hindus, the foreignness of the Christian theology to the philosophic background of Hinduism--all of these possibly were the contributing factors. However, it is equally important that all the above Hindu thinkers saw in Jesus Christ the embodiment of their own ideals which to them was not different from Hinduism.

Kesab Sen saw in Jesus the example of supreme self-surrender. For Vivekânanda Jesus is Jivanmukta (who has achieved freedom when alive); for Gandhi he is the supreme Satyâgrahi (lover and fighter of truth). Each of the Hindu Thinkers could incorporate Christ in their own religious framework and not feel any need to renounce their own religion. They found no difference between Jesus' teaching and the 'Sanâtana Dharma' (the perennial truth). It was not seen as a really New Testament, a New Gospel, but the restatement of the eternal. The different Christian Churches, according to these Hindu thinkers, are different Sects of religion and they have the right to exist just as the different sects of Hinduism also exist. As Hindus they were tolerant of the different religious sects, but they denounced the proselytizing of

73

the Christian missionaries. This seemed to them
to be a product of sectarianism and therefore
deplorable. The Hindus admired Christ. They
wrote about him with admiration. Some Hindu
writers attempted to give a systematic account of
the Hindu view of Christ. For example,
Akhilananda wrote Hindu View of Christ. S. P.
Radhakrishnan in his Eastern Religion and Western
Thought presented a Hindu understanding of
Christ, which to him is the authentic understanding as opposed to the distorted understanding of the West. By analyzing these accounts as well as the writings of Hindu renaissance leaders like Rammohan Roy, Vivekānananda
and Gandhi we can notice certain well marked
trends in these Hindu writer's understanding of
Christ. First, the Hindu writers understood
Christ in terms of his ethical teachings.
Second, they identified Jesus as one of the
avatars. Third, they understood Jesus in mystical terms. They understood him in terms of
identity of Ātman and Brahman. They referred to
the cosmic Christ rather than the historical
Jesus. Jesus for them is an embodiment of a
universal principle rather than a distinctive
individual. Because Christ represents something
universal, he cannot be identified with the
Western form of it. Christianity has to be
dissociated from Western 'Churchianity.' With the
exception of Rammohan Roy, almost all the Hindu
thinkers emphasized the Gospel of John and the
mystical epistles of Paul.

Ethical Understanding of Christ

        Jesus' ethical teachings impressed most of
the Hindu thinkers. Rājā Rammohan Roy, the
pioneer of the liberal reform of Hindu religion
and society, published The Precepts of Jesus The
Guide to Peace and Happiness Extracted from the
Books of the New Testament, ascribed to the four
Evangelists (with translations into Sanskrit and
Bengalise) in 1820. This book, a collection of
Jesus' ethical teachings, was meant for Hindu
people in general. The book contained the
Sermons and the Parables and left out the doctri-
nal teachings or historical accounts. Rammohan
Roy was a liberal rationalist. To him Hindu
polytheism and the corrupt social practices in
India were intolerable. He associated the two.
According to him reason justifies monotheism and
the corollary of monotheism is "do unto others as

ye would be done."[12] In Jesus' teachings he found
a representation of his ideal of religion which
combines rationalism and morality. In one of his
letters to Mr. John Digby in 1815 he wrote, "The
consequence of my long and uninterrupted resear-
ches into religious truth has been that I have
found the doctrine of Christ more conducive to
moral principles and better adapted to the use of
rational beings than any other which have come to
my knowledge."[13]

Moral teaching, according to Rammohan Roy,
is the essence of Christianity. Therefore, he
selected from the synoptic Gospels and left the
fourth Gospel out because of its obvious doctrinal and speculative nature. The reason for the
separation and selection of the ethical teachings
is,

> Moral doctrines...are beyond the reach of
> metaphysical perversion and intelligible
> alike to the learned and the unlearned. This
> simple code of religion and morality is so
> admirably calculated to elevate man's ideas
> to high and liberal notions of God, who has
> equally submitted all living creatures,
> without distinction of caste, rank or wealth
> to change, disappointment, pain and death and
> has equally admitted all to be partakers of
> the bountiful mercies which he has lavished
> over nature and is also so well fitted to
> regulate the conduct of the human race in the
> discharge of their various duties to them-
> selves and to society...."[14]

Rammohan Roy was acquainted with the liberal
Protestants of his time. Albert Schweitzer's The
Quest of Historical Jesus was yet to appear.
However, that critical attitude was in the
atmosphere. Rammohan Roy was also aware of the
doctrinal controversies among the Christians.
While he was helping a Serampore missionary,
William Adams, in his translation of the Gospel
of John, Rammohan Roy observed how Adams and
another collaborator landed in a trinitan's
controversy in their translation of the prologue.
Ultimately Adams professed unitarianism.
Rammohan Roy, therefore, felt he was justified in
thinking that the historical and doctrinal
teachings of the Gospels were controversial,
whereas the moral teaching was undisputable and
simple and could elevate humans. Therefore,

although he emphasized the moral teachings he did
not say much about the nature of the teacher.
However, Rammohan Roy's "precepts" gave rise to a
heated controversy between him and the Serampore
missionary Joshua Marshman.[15] In the course of
this controversy Roy spelled out his understanding of the nature of Jesus Christ.

Marshman's opposition came to Roy as a shock
as his understanding of Christianity was in
concord within liberal Protestants that he knew.
Marshman was annoyed by the separation of the
ethical from historical and soterelogical.
However, because of the way Marshman handled the
controversy, it became theological and metaphysical. He was trying to prove that the later
theological developed doctrines were explicitly
present in the Bible. From his arguments and
objections to Roy it seemed that a simple faith
response to the Gospel was not enough but that a
confession of a creed was mandatory.

Rammohan Roy was looking at Jesus from his
Hindu perspective. According to the Hindu
tradition, ultimately the teaching is important,
not the teacher. The teacher is venerated as
God--_acarya_ _deva_ _bhava_ ("teacher is God"). From
the advaitic perspective, the teacher and the
teaching may not be two; yet for the theist
Rammohan Roy, they are distinct and have to be
kept distinct. For Roy the identity of nature
between Jesus and God was incomprehensible--it
was totally illogical. For him it was also
repulsive because it made the Christian doctrine
indistinguishable from Hindu polytheism and
idolatry. He quoted extensively from the Bible
to show that the Son is inferior to the Father.[16]
The identity passages of the Bible, Rammohan Roy
interpreted, as identity of will and not of
Being.

He said that the clue for understanding
appeared in the identity passages in Jesus'
teaching of the identity between Him and the
Father and between him and the apostles. If the
identity in both instances is of a nature then
there can be only three ways of understanding it.

First, as conveying the doctrine that the
Supreme Being, the Son and the Apostles were
to be absorbed mutually as drops of water
into one whole; which is conformable to the

76

doctrine of that sect of Hindoo metaphysicians which maintains that in the end the human soul is absorbed into the Godhead; but is quite inconsistent with the faith of all denominations of Christians. Secondly, as proving an identity of nature, with distinction of person, between the Father, the Son and the Apostles, a doctrine equally inconsistent with the belief of every Christian, as multiplying the number of the persons of the Godhead far beyond what has been proposed by any sect.

Thirdly, as expressing that unity which is said to exist whenever there are found perfect concord, harmony, love and obedience such as the Son evinced towards the Father, and taught the disciple to display towards the Divine Will. That the language of the Savior can be understood in this last sense solely, will, I trust, be readily acknowledged by every candid expounder of the sacred writings, as being the only one alike warranted by the common use of the words, and capable of apprehension by the human understanding.[17]

Roy was willing to accept Jesus as superior to all other humans. Jesus was the first born, yet a creature and not identical with God. He was the Messiah as sent by God; the mediator giving the message of God to humanity. He was not the Savior in the transcendental Christian understanding of atonement, but as a teacher. For Roy vicarious suffering is opposed to the principle of justice. He held that the sacrifice model of the cross was presented by Jesus to communicate to the Jews in their own terminology.[18] In the same way the Trinitarian understanding of the Godhead is a concession to Gentile polytheism,[19] but not justified either from the perspective of reason or Christian monotheism.[20] Roy saw in the Christian notion of Incarnation a parallel to the Hindu idea of Thākur (avatar), because both are founded on the same sacred basis viz., the manifestation of God in flesh.[21] He displayed an Islamic disgust to such an idea. He said it is no better than Hindu polytheism. Both are equally and solely protected by the "shield of mystery."[22]

77

M. C. Gandhi, like Rammohan Roy, was attracted to Jesus's moral teachings, particularly the idea of "resist no evil." Gandhi believed in the rightness and value of passive resistance. He was thrilled when in the 'Sermon on the Mount' he found the confirmation of his belief.[23] According to Gandhi the essence of any religion is its moral teaching and the epitome of moral teaching is 'Ahimsa' ("non-violence"). Ahimsa alone can lead men and women to truth which, in the long run, is the only valid object of veneration. In his prayer songs he used to sing about the non-distinction of Rāma and Rahim, Allah and Iśvara. However, whenever he spoke about God he was more comfortable in speaking in terms of principles than of person, in terms of truth rather than of any personality.

I do not regard God as person. Truth for me is God, and God's law and God are not different things or facts in the sense that earthly King and his law are different. Because God is an idea, Law Himself... Not a blade of grass grows or moves without His will.[24]

In the background of his idea about religion and God, Gandhi understood Jesus as a supremely moral person and as an impressive moral teacher who taught his precepts more by example of his personality than by any preaching. Gandhi, like Rammohan Roy emphasized the teachings not the teacher. The historicity of Jesus is not important, but his "Sermon" is. "I may say that I have never been interested in a historical Jesus. I should not care if it was proved by some man called Jesus ever lived, and that was narrated in the Gospels was a figment of the writer's imagination. For the Sermon on the Mount would still be true to me."[25] Gandhi, like Roy, did not accept the vicarious atonement understanding of the cross. For Roy the cross represents total obedience. Gandhi found in it the symbol of eternal re-occurrence of death and resurrection of moral struggle of humanity. According to Gandhi human life is a life of moral struggle for peace and happiness. In order to achieve this there is need of sacrifice of the egocentric man. The cross represents this sacrifice of the ego. This is a continuous process.

Roy found vicarious expiation of sin unjust.
Gandhi saw in it an element of endorsement of
licentiousness. His attitude can be compared to
Luther's indignation at the selling of indulgences. The Plymouth Brethren in England whom
Gandhi encountered, used to argue that Christians
can do whatever they want, because Jesus has
suffered and atoned for all sins of humankind.
This to Gandhi was obnoxious. He looked upon
human life as an experiment with truth according
to moral principles. His concern was not so much
about the consequences of sin as for sin itself.
Asking for forgiveness of sin, as Jesus taught in
the Gospel, meant a change of heart so as not to
sin again. Gandhi was also unhappy about Indian
Christians' beef eating and alcohol drinking. To
his disapproval the Indian Christian used to
quote from the Scriptures that nothing should be
considered unclean. Gandhi considered this a
distortion of Jesus' teaching.[26]

Gandhi acknowledged Jesus as a great religious teacher. Unlike Roy, he could even accept
him as one of the Avatāra. However, to think
that Jesus was the only true teacher or the only
Incarnation of God was not possible for him. He
argued that history showed there were many
religious teachers. To evaluate their relative
merit on the basis of historical facts is not
possible. Historical data about all are not
equally available. About Mohammed we know the
most, of Kṛṣṇa the least. "To say that Jesus was
ninety per cent divine and Mohammed fifty per
cent and Kṛṣṇa ten per cent is to arrogate to
oneself a function which really does not belong
to man. We must consider all prophets even Moses
and Jesus as equal. It is a horizontal plane."[27]
According to Gandhi all religions are equal in
the sense of being imperfect, human ways of
grasping the Truth and reflecting the same spirit
of Truth. This is evident in the similarity of
ethical teachings of all religions.

According to Gandhi Jesus cannot be the only
begotten son of God. "If God could have sons,
all of us were his sons. If Jesus was like God,
or God himself, then all men were like God or
could be God Himself."[28] Though Gandhi was not a
Vedāntin, he spoke like a Vedāntin, as any Hindu
in one way or another does.

79

Avatāra Understanding of Christ

In the ethical understanding of Jesus by Roy and Gandhi, the emphasis is on the humanity of Jesus. In the Avatāra understanding the emphasis is on the divinity of Christ. Jesus Christ was presented as an Avatāra by Rāmkrishna Paramahamsa. The writings of the monks of Rāmkrisha order are in the same spirit. Akhilananda's Hindu View of Christ is a systematic account of such an understanding. Vivekānanda spoke about Christ as an Avatāra. However, his understanding is more mystical and has influenced Radhakrishnan's mystical understanding of Christ.

Rāmkrishna's exposure to Christianity was through the Hindu, Jadu Mallick, who worshipped Jesus as his 'Ista.' He read parts of the Bible to Rāmkrishna. A summary of Rāmakrishna's direct experience of Christ is given in the Gospel of Rāmakrishna.[29] One day as he was sitting in Jadu Mallick's house his eyes became fixed on the picture of the Madonna and Child and he was overwhelmed with a sense of the divine. He was in ecstacy. The Christian writers usually describe Rāmakrisha's ecstacy as a trance and death-like state. From the Hindu perspective it was an encounter with reality; Rāmakrishna was in direct communion with the reality of Jesus; Jesus possessed his soul. For three days he did not go to the Kāli Temple. In the fourth day when he was walking along the bank of Ganges "he saw coming towards him a person with beautiful large eyes, serene countenance and fair skin."[30] This may not be an accurate picture of the historical Jesus as might now be suggested by historical researchers, but this is how Jesus is visualized by humans in general. Rāmakrishna had the vision of Jesus and an inner voice told him: "Behold the Christ who shed his heart's blood for the redemption of the world, who suffered a sea of anguish for love of men. It is He, the master yogi, who is in eternal union with God. It is Jesus, Love Incarnate." They embraced each other and Jesus merged into Rāmakrisha. Nikhilānanda, the writer of the introduction of The Gospel of Rāmkrisha, writes further that:

Ramakrishna realized his identity with Christ, as he has already realized his identity with Kāli, Rāma, Hanumāna, Rādha,

80

Krishna, Brahman and Muhammad...thus he
experienced that Christianity, too, was a
path leading to God-consciousness. Till the
last moment of his life he believed that
Christ was in Incarnation of God. But
Christ, for him, was not the only Incarnation; there were others, Buddha, for instance, and Krishna.[31]

The Hindu belief in Avatàra is quite ancient.
It shows some parallel to the Christian notion of
Incarnation. Some Christian scholars of the
nineteenth and twentieth centuries, e.g.,
Albrecht Weber, suggested that the avatàra idea
of Hinduism is borrowed from Christianity.[32]
However, Parrindar repudiates this view. He says
that the influence of Christianity on Hinduism
before nineteenth century cannot be proved by any
scholarly method. Besides, according to him the
Avatàra doctrine is fully Indian. By recounting
the history of this doctrine in Hinduism he shows
that the idea was present in the Mahàbhàrata and
not only in its section of the Gità. It developed through the Purànas into Vaisnavism and was
helped by Ràmànuja's philosophical discourse.
All along it was a natural and spontaneous
development from the epics.[33] In contemporary
Christian scholarship the tendency is to emphasize the distinction between Hindu idea of
Avatàra and Christian notion of Incarnation,
e.g., H. Zimmer.[34]

Panikkar also emphasizes the difference
between the two.[35] However, many Hindu writers
look upon Jesus as an Avatàra. According to
Avatàra Christology Jesus Christ is fully divine.
Vivekànanda says, "If as an oriental I have to
worship Jesus of Nazareth there is only one way
left to me, that is to worship him as God and
nothing else."[36] Hindus from this perspective
emphasize the extraordinary qualities of Jesus,
which in turn lead to the many psychiatric
investigations of Jesus' life by some nineteenth
century psychiatrists. Albert Schweitzer's The
Psychiatric Study of Jesus was a response to
them. This book is a defense against the psychiatric conclusion that Jesus was psychotic.
His main argument is that the psychiatrists
depended mainly on the Gospel of John to prove
their theory, but that the Gospel of John is not
historically authentic. Akhilànanda in the Hindu
view of Christ argues that Schweitzer's defense

does not touch the root of the problem. Jesus is extraordinary, but there is a gulf of difference between the extraordinary characteristics of Jesus and the abnormalities of a psychotic. Rāmakrishna also referred to the extraordinary qualities of the incarnations:

> They are human beings with extra ordinary, original powers and entrusted with a divine commission. Being heirs of divine power and glories they form a class of their own. To this class belong the incarnations of God like Christ, Krishna, Buddha and Caitanya and devotees of higher order.[37]

Akhilānanda claims that as incarnation Jesus had full knowledge of his mission. That is why he could speak with authority. Jesus also displayed the extraordinary love and compassion of the incarnation as well. Knowing fully well that Judas was going to betray him he did not take away his blessings from him. On the cross he could pray for the forgiveness of his persecutors. Avatāras by their love and grace can save their followers. Although the vicarious atonement of sin is not accepted with its Christian meaning, it is indicated that Avatāras can take upon themselves the consequences of karma of others and suffer in their stead. Rāmakrishna's suffering from cancer is usually interpreted by his devotees in this way. Rāmakrishna said,

> When a mighty log of wood floats down the stream, it carries on it hundreds of birds and does not sink.... So when a Savior incarnates, innumerable are men who find salvation by taking refuge in him.[38]

According to Hindu idea of Avatāra there are special reasons for God's descent in the world. The Bhāgavad Gitā says:

> Whenever dharma declines and adharma preponders, in order to save the good and destroy evil and to reestablish dharma I take on flesh time and again.[39]

Akhilananda indicates that Jesus was born for similar reasons. Judaism became corrupt. Paganism was equally deplorable. Akhilānanda by quoting Matthew 11:27 notes that Jesus came to the world to teach the humans about God and their

82

own true being. Therefore Jesus also came to reestablish dharma. Some Hindus consider Jesus as Avatàra. He is not the only Avatàra. Ràmakrishna said:

It is one and the same avatàra that being plunged into the ocean of life, rises up in one place and is known as Krishna, and diving again rises in another place and is known as Christ.[40]

The Avatàra Christology emphasizes the divinity of Christ almost exclusively. It does not take too much account of the passion of Gathsamene or the death on the cross. Vivekànabda said: "Christ was God incarnate; they could not kill him. That which was crucified was only a resemblance, a mirage."[41] Akhilananda quoting Phil 2:6-7 indicates that Paul, like the Hindus, had the understanding that when God incarnates, he deliberately imposes on himself some limitations, yet he is God and remains a God. Akhilananda introduces his book by quoting John's prologue--"In the beginning was the Word." The eternity and the pre-existence of the incarnate Word is so emphasized that "The word was made flesh" is interpreted in an almost totally docetic way.

The Mystical Understanding of Christ

The Mystical Understanding of Christ also is based on the fourth Gospel--and entirely on the "identity" statements of the Gospel--plus Paul's "mystical" utterances. The motif of the Hindu mystical understanding of Christ is provided by Jesus' saying, "The Father and I are one," and Paul's saying, "It is not I but Christ lives in me."

This mystical understanding of Christ is systematically presented by S. P. Radhakrishnan in his "Eastern Religion and Western Thought," whose view was molded by Vivekananda, as he noted in an autobiographical essay.[42] Having studied under the conservative missionary Hogg, Radhankrishnan was acquainted with the exclusivistic version of Christianity as well as the Christian criticism of Hinduism. Consequently, the Eastern Religion and Western Thought was a critique of Western Christianity and an apologetic for Hinduism.

83

According to Radhakrishnan Jesus taught an universal perennial truth which is in concord with Snāntana dharma. However, the Western attitude transformed the universalistic teaching of Jesus into an exclusivistic dogmatic creed with its consequent intolerance. The formulation of the Nicene creed was the victory of Rome over the Christian Gospel.

The Roman empire failed to destroy Christianity by persecution, but the hour of her victory over Rome signified the defeat of the Gospel of Jesus. Christianity became bound up with the civilization under which it grew. The church became the depository of Sacred Wisdom, a sort of reservoir of theological secrets and not a spring.[43]

Radhakrishnan criticizes Schweitzer and Heiler for their either/or distinction between prophetic world-affirming and mystical world-denying religions. According to him, Schweitzer and Heiler's version of prophetic religion "have more in common with non-pagan faiths than with the self-denying, self-forgetful genius of Christianity whose symbol is the cross."[44]

The cross signifies abandonment of the ego and identification with a fuller life and consciousness. The soul is raised to a universal level.

"In Gethsemane, Christ as an individual felt that the cup should pass away. That was his personal desire. The secret of the cross is the crucifixion of the ego and the yielding to the will of God. 'Thy will be done'."[45]

Like Gandhi, Radhakrishnan also does not emphasize the historic event but interprets it as a symbol. However, for Gandhi the cross represents the moral struggle which for him is equivalent to spirituality. For RadhaKrishnan spirituality is understood more in Vedàntic mystical terms rather than as moral struggle.

Resurrection also is understood in the similar way. It is not raising of the corpse from the tomb. It is,

...the passage from the death of self-absorption to the life of unselfish love, the

84

transition from the darkness of selfish
individualism to the light of universal
spirit, from falsehood to truth, from slavery
to the world to the liberty of the eternal.[46]

Jesus' death and resurrection should not be
interpreted just as mere events of history which
happened once upon a time. They represent a
universal process of spiritual life which is
being continuously accomplished in the soul of
men and women. Christhood is an attainment of a
state of the soul. This seems to be an echo of
Vivekānanda's statement, "Jesus had our nature:
he became Christ; so can we, so must we. Christ
and Buddha were names of states to be attained.
Jesus and Gautama were the persons to manifest
it."[47] According to this mystical understanding
of Christ, incarnation is the realization of the
supreme potentiality of humanity which is not
different from divinity. Vivekānanda said that
human Jesus realized his true nature--his divinity and realized the truth that

> Every man and woman, whether Jew or Greek,
> whether rich or poor, whether saint or
> sinner, was the embodiment of the same
> underlying Spirit as himself. Therefore, the
> one work his whole life showed, was calling
> upon them to realize their own spiritual
> nature.... You are all sons of God, Immortal
> spirit. 'Know' he declared, 'the kingdom of
> Heaven is within you.' 'I and my Father are
> One.'[48]

Thus, according to the mystical understanding of
Jesus, like the ethical understanding of him, he
is looked upon more as an example than as an
ontological mediator or as a sotereological
savior. His role is the role of a teacher.
Vivekānanda indicated that as a genuine teacher
he taught the truth according to the capabilities
and the requirements of the taught. For some he
taught Lord's prayer. For other disciples he
taught, "I in my Father, and ye in me, and I in
you." When asked about his own nature he said, "I
and my Father are one."That, according to
Vivekānanda, was the teaching of the prophets
also. They said, "Ye are Gods and all of you are
Children of the Most High." For Vivekānanda,
Jesus' teaching is not different from teachings
of Vedānta. Radhakrishnan also believes that
Jesus' teaching is Vedāntic. Although in the

85

later developed Christianity, Jesus' teaching is
primarily understood in terms of its Jewish
context; it has the universal message of a
religion as inner experience, as love and tolerance. Jesus did not teach any religion of
external rituals or legalistic piety, but he
believed in inner light and direct religious
experience. He did not claim any newness in his
teachings, did not want to organize any group or
formulate any creed. He did not distinguish
between the Jews and the Gentiles, Romans and
Greeks. He taught how one can deepen ones
spirituality and live a life of higher quality
than is not usually lived by humans. Jesus
"proclaims love of God or insight into the nature
of reality, and love of man's oneness with the
purpose of the universe, as the central truth of
religion."49

Christian Responses

     In the panorama of Christian Christological
thinking there are evidences of de-emphasis of
historical Jesus (Bultman), emphasis on his
ethical teachings (Harnach) and emphasis on
cosmic Christ (Rahner). It is not impossible to
find parallels to the different Hindu idea of
Jesus Christ and some Christian understanding of
him. The Christian contemporaries of the above
Hindu thinkers, however, responded very negatively to such understanding of Christ, although
many among them were positively impressed and
influenced by some of them. C. F. Andrews,
Stanley Jones were positively influenced by
Gandhi. Andrews opposed mass conversion and
creedal rigidity. He even ultimately resigned
from priesthood when he heard Indian choir boys
chanting the Athanesian creed. He related how
his being with Gandhi during his historic fast in
Delhi helped him understand the deeper meaning of
the cross. Stanley Jones indicated that Gandhi
helped him understand the true spirit of Christianity. He almost said that Gandhi is an
'anonymous Christian.' He compared Gandhi's
assassination to the tragedy of the cross. "Never
did a death more fittingly crown a life, save
only one--the son of God."50 Gandhi's influence
on the Christian thinking of the time became very
evident in the Tambarama conference in Madras in
1938. A. G. Hogg, who was one of the important
figures of conservative Christianity, spoke of
the incarnation as the transcendent satyàgraha of

God. Eric Sharpe indicated how deeply Gandhi influenced twentieth century Protestant thought in general and the "Rethinking Christianity" group in India in particular. Some claimed him as their own, others thought that if he is an adherent of Hinduism it must have some merit.

Christians did not come into direct contact with Rāmakrishna. His teachings as it is interpreted by Vivekānanda, posed a challenge to Christianity. This stimulated Christian thinking. Volumes of literature have been produced by the Christian writers referring to Vedānta and Christianity. Vivekānanda received wide welcome in America in 1893. He established the seeds of many Vedānta centers in West specially in England and America. Through him the West came to know of yato mata tato patha--"there are as many ways to God as there are different views." This stimulated the spirit of ecumenism.

The nature and vehemence of criticism of the different Christian thinkers concerning the Hindu thinkers were not the same. Marshman's opposition to Rammohan Roy was the most vehement. However, Roy's precepts were instrumental in the conversion of some important Hindus to Christianity, for example, M. N. Bose and M. C. Parekh. Certain trends seem to be common in the criticisms. All the Christians respondents were concerned about the de-emphasis on history. For them Jesus is a definitive event of history and is to be so understood. C. F. Andrews spoke sarcastically about the Hindu idea that whether or not Christ or Kṛṣṇa really existed it makes no difference, for thosé who conceived of a Christ or a Kṛṣṇa must have lived like them. Andrews remarked that it needs a Christ to forge a Christ; the thinkers who conjured up the image of Kṛṣṇa perhaps were as great or as moral as the Kṛṣṇa they conceived. Obviously he was referring to the Vrindāvana lilā, the erotic understanding of which can shock the moral sense of a Christian with an Augustinian idea of concupiscence. Secondly, the Christian thinkers were dissatisfied with the separation of ethical and soteriological. This is very prominent in Marshman's opposition to Rammohan. Thirdly, the Christians objected to the selection and interpretation of Bible out of their contexts. This was Marshman's chief objection to Rammohan Roy. Andrews, in The Renaissance India: Its Missionary Aspect,

sionary Aspect, complained that by separating the
Johanine Gospel from the rest of Bible tradition
the neo-Vedānta of Vivekānanda gave the fourth
Gospel a strange interpretation.

Panikkar's Christological thinking and the possible responses from the perspectives of the Hindu thinkers

The purpose of this chapter is not to
determine the authenticity of the different
understandings of Christ by the above Hindu
thinkers. Panikkar in the article, "The relationship of Gospel to Hindu Religion and Culture," says that the figure of the oriental
Christ that emerged from the renaissance Bengal
in the last century is obviously different from
the Western image of Jesus, but "where is the
criterion to set the criterion to know whether
they were deforming the image of the saviour?"
Panikkar therefore does not criticize any of
these understandings of Christ although he would
perhaps disagree with many of the Hindu thinkers'
contentions. At least he cannot agree with
understanding Jesus Christ simply in terms of his
ethical teaching, or with considering him as
either only human or only divine. He clearly
indicates the differences between the Hindu idea
of avatāra and the idea of Christ as the ontological and soteriological mediator. Yet Panikkar
in his theological thinking addressed himself to
the issues that have been raised by the Hindu
understanding of Christ. He repeatedly mentions
the limitation of identifying Christianity with
its Western mediterranean form. He says that it
is Western colonialism and totalitarianism that
underlies the attempt to translate everything in
Judeo-Greco-Modern categories.

> Thus Asia, for example, compelled to speak in
> some European language, will have to say
> 'way' instead of Tao, 'God' instead of
> Brahman and 'soul' instead of atman; it must
> translate dharma as 'justice,' chan as
> 'meditation,' and so forth.[51]

Just as such Asian terms cannot be properly
translated in English terminology and to understand them one has to go to their deeper meaning,
so the Gospel of Christ can not be meaningful to
the non-Westerners if it is
delivered in terms of Western Christianity and
not in terms of its inner significance. If it is

said to the Indians that Jesus is the Messiah it would not be meaningful to them as like the Jews they were not expecting any Messiah. In the same way if Jesus is described as son of God, a Vedāntin would reply 'so are we.' The relationship of religion and culture is a serious issue for any religion which claims to have a universal message for the whole of humanity.

The different Hindu thinkers have clearly indicated the limitations of understanding Christianity and Christ in simple historical terms. Panikkar takes note of it and says that to identify Christ with Jesus of Nazareth, an individual understood in terms of spatio-temporal coordinates, would amount to idolatry.

The freezing of the ineffable supreme in one particular object of senses or of mind, is said to be the greatest sin against the spirit.[52]

We have noted in Ch. III how Panikkar indicated that identification of Christ with historical Jesus would make many Christian confessions of faith, as well as many sacraments, ridiculous. Panikkar wants to distinguish between individuality and personality. Individuals as spatio-temporal points cannot be unique, but person as network of relationship can.

As a Christian, Panikkar considers Godhood in personalistic terms, although his notion of personhood is different from the understanding of it in substantive terms which is usually represented by the term, homoousios. However, he agrees with the above-mentioned Hindu thinkers that the Ultimate is infinite and ineffable. Therefore, he talks about the apophatic element of Godhead and the non-personal aspect of Godhead in his understanding of God as the Father and God as the Spirit.

Panikkar clearly indicates the difference between the Hindu idea of avatāra and the Christian understanding of Christ. Hindu avatāra is a soteriological mediator. Christian Christ is also an ontological mediator. Panikkar indicates that Christ is more analogous to the advaita vedāntic notion of Iśvara than to avatāras of viṣṇu. However, as in the avatāra understanding, he believes in the possibility of there being

89

saviors other than Jesus. Christ is fully
expressed in Jesus, but there can be other
Christophanies, and Krsna or Gautama need not be
excluded.

Interpretation of Bible by the different
Hindu thinkers highlights the hermeneutic problem. The text is understood according to ones
context. The different Hindu thinkers understood
Bible from their Hindu contexts. Panikkar
therefore asks the question, 'what is the criterion to set the criteria?' He thinks that contemporary interpretation of Bible has to be in terms
of its global context. The contemporary context
necessitates a more universalistic and inclusivistic interpretation than an understanding of it
in terms of exclusion--opposition to all the
other messages. Panikkar says that the Wester-
ner's emphasis on the law of contradiction makes
it inevitable for them to understand everything
in terms of contrast, in terms of opposition,
whereas Indian emphasis on law of identity.
stimulates an inclusivistic understanding of
things.

It is evident that Panikkar was dealing with
the issues raised by the different Hindu think-
ings about Christ. It is also evident that his
interpretation of Christianity, or his Christian
thinking, can be better understood from the
perspectives of the different Hindu thinkers
than, for example, from traditional Augustinian
or Thomistic perspectives, even though Panikkar
himself has Thomistic elements in his thinking.
From the perspectives of the different Hindu
thinkers, particularly of Vivekānanda and
Radhakrishnan, it is possible to respond positively to Panikkar's understanding of Christ as
the ontological mediator, Church as the mystical
body of Christ and thus inclusive of whole
humanity, and his idea of a universal religion
which he names as Christianity without denying
the possibility of calling it by other names.
The Hindu thinkers can respond positively to all
the universalistic elements of Panikkar's thinking. However, Panikkar also insists that the
universal is also concrete. Christ is not only
cosmic he is also historical. Church can be
co-extensive with humanity yet it is visible.
The universal Religion is not a Platonic essence
but gets incarnated in different historical
forms. The Hindu thinkers, particularly the

90

advaitins, would insist that the universal is more real than the concrete, the perfection of history cannot be in history. The universal is made concrete in history, no doubt, yet every historical manifestation falls short of the perfection of the universal. The Sanãtana dharma, the perennial order is manifested in pluralistic forms. None of these forms, individually or together, can be a perfect expression of it. Panikkar, on the other hand, thinks that all the pluralistic forms of religion insofar as they are true would reach their culmination in a concrete form in the universal religion. They would not lose their concrete distinctiveness by this process and merge in an abstract totality. He wants to maintain both concreteness and universality at the same time. How that can be in reality he cannot specify. He is aware of the theoretical problems of joining the concrete with its particularity and the universal, but thinks it possible: He says that:

> The fact that the Church is visible does not imply that its limits are visible to everybody or anybody. Precisely because she is visible she presents the possibility of different limits of visibility. Whereas some do not see much beyond their Church yard, other, encompass a wider horizon. To affirm that her confines touch the very limits of mankind--without saying that they coalesce--does not contradict the visibility of the church.[53]

From the way that Panikkar presents his case, it may seem that like Vivekãnanda he also says that different people are on different levels of spirituality. Yet it must be indicated that as a Catholic he believes in parusia, a stage where every human being would have the widest vision of reality; the Hindu thinkers do not believe in any supralapsarism. For them world is the realm of karma. World is for acting out ones salvation. The major point of difficulty between Hindu-Catholic dialogue seems to be their attitudinal differences towards the world. The fundamental question is, what is the status of the world and the individual human beings of the world in their relationship with the ultimate reality? In the following chapter we shall discuss the world views of the two important schools of Vedãnta which represents the world

views of the Hindu thinkers and, by way of
comparison of them with Panikkar's cosmo-theandrism, try to investigate whether the Vedāntic
Hindu and the Catholic world views are really
incompatible or not.

Notes

Panikkar and Some Hindu Views About Christ and
Christianity

[1] Panikkar, "The Relationship of Gospels to
Hindu Culture and Religion," in Jesus and Man's
Hope. Vol. 2, p. 252.

[2] Stephen Neill, The Story of the Christian
Church in India and Pakistan (Grand Rapids:
Eordmans, 1970).

[3] Jadu Mallick, for example, was a lay
disciple of Ràmakrishna and accepted Jesus as his
chosen deity. He is referred to in Gospel of
Ràmakrishna, with an Introduction by
Nikhilànanda, trans. (N.Y. Ràmakrishna
Vivekànanda Centre, 1973).

[4] Keshab Sen is quoted in M. C. Parekh,
Brahmarshi Kesab Chandra Sen (Rajkot: Oriental
Christ House, 1926), p. 104.

[5] Ibid., p. 160.

[6] Kesabsen is quoted in Romain Rolland,
Prophets of New India, p. 1, Life of Ramakrishna
(New York, 1930), publisher's note, p. 291 ff,
quoted in M. M. Thomas in The Acknowledged Christ
of the Indian Renaissance (London: SCM, 1969),
p. 114-115.

[7] Vivekànanda, The Complete Works, 5th ed.
(Almora Mayavati Advaita Ashrama, 1931), vol. 3,
pp. 182-186.

[8] Swami Prabhavànanda, The Sermon on The
Mount According to Vedànta (N.Y.:   Mentor, 1972),
p. xiv.

[9] Harijan, May 25, 1935, quoted in M. M.
Thomas, op. cit., p. 194.

[10] M. K. Gandhi, The Message of Jesus Christ
(Ahmedabad, 1940), p. 79, quoted in M. M. Thomas,
p. 199.

[11] Id., Christian Missions (Ahmedabad,
1940), p. 23, quoted in M. M. Thomas, p. 198.

[12] English Works of Raja Rammohan Roy. Panini Office, Bahadurganj, Allahabad, 1960. Reprint: N.Y. AMS Press, 1978.

[13] Quoted in M. M. Thomas, The Acknowledged Christ, pp. 8-9.

[14] English Works of Rammohan Roy, pp. 484 ff.

[15] History of the Controversy in M. M. Thomas, Ch. 1. See also its bibliography.

[16] Rammohan, English Works, pp. 573-77.

[17] Ibid., p. 578.

[18] Ibid., pp. 700-75.

[19] Ibid., p. 629.

[20] Ibid., p. 632.

[21] Ibid., p. 892.

[22] Ibid., p. 172.

[23] Gandhi Message, p. 3.

[24] Id., Harijan, quoted in Thomas, p. 194.

[25] Id., Message, p. 35.

[26] Ibid., p. 1.
[27] Ibid., p. 51.

[28] Ibid., p. 34.

[29] For details of Rāmakrishna's life, see Gambhirananda Sri Rāmakrishna and His Unique Message (London: Vedanta Centre, 1970). There are many works on him by Christian authors: E. G. Romain Rolland, Life of Ramakrishna (N.Y., 1930); Nalini Devadas, Sri Rama Krishna (Bangalore, 1965).

[30] Gospel of Ramakrishna, p. 34.

[31] Ibid., p. 34.

[32] Parrinder, Avatara and Incarnation

(Princeton: a Bollinger Series, Princeton, 1969), p. 117.

33 Ibid., p. 117.

34 H. Zimmer, Philosophies of India (Princeton: Princeton U.Press, Bollinger Series, 1971).

35 R. Panikkar, The Unknown Christ of Hinduism. Here he shows that Christ is comparable to Iśvara not to Avatāra.

36 Vivekānanda, Complete Works, vol. 4, p. 143.

37 The Gospel of Ramakrishna, revised by Swami Abhedananda, New York: The Vedanta Society, 1947, p. 300-301, quoted in Akhilananda Hindu View of Christ, p. 20.

38 Sayings of Ramakrishna, 3rd ed. (Sri Ramakrishna Math Mylapore Madras, 1925), p. 140. Quoted in Akhilamada. p. 23-24.

39 Bhagabad Gita, 4:7, 8.

40 Max Müller, Ramakrishna: His Life and Sayings. p. 52, quoted in Thomas, p. 121.

41 Vivekananda, Complete Works 4, p. 144.

42 Radhakrishnan, "My Search for Truth," in Religion in Transition, ed. Vergalius Ferm (London, 1937), p. 15.

43 Radhakrishnan, "Eastern Religion and Western Thought," in Christianity: Some non-Christian Appraisals, ed. McKain (N.Y.: McGraw Hill, 1964) p.28

44 Radhakrishnan., Eastern Religion and Western Thought, p. 66.

45 Ibid., p. 97.

46 Ibid., p. 47.

47 Vivekananda, Complete Works, vol. 7, pp. 20,27

48 Ibid., vol. 4, pp. 141 ff.

49 Radhakrishnan, "Eastern Religion and Western Thought," in _Christianity_, ed. McKain, p. 26.

50 Stanley Jones is quoted in M. M. Thomas, _The_ _Acknowledged_ _Christ_ _of_ _Hindu_ _Renaissance_, p. 226.

51 Panikkar, _Intrereligious_ _Dialogue_, p. 3.

52 Panikkar, _Salvation_ _in_ _Christ_. p. 41.

53 Panikkar Ibid., p. 15.

Chapter 5

Vedānta and Panikkar

Radhakrishanan quite clearly states: "In one or the other of its forms the Vedānta determines the world view of the Hindu thinkers of the present time."[1] The different Hindu thinkers' views of Christianity and Christ discussed in the last chapter have the vedāntic world view. The renascent Hindu thinkers believe that Hinduism can be revitalized through Vedānta. Vivekānanda talked about practical Vedānta in so far as it can remove superstition and narrow ritualism. Swāmi Sivānanda, a follower of practical Vedānta said:

> Vedānta is the basic culture of India. It is the national philosophy of India. It is the summit or peak or acme of Indian philosophy. It kept Hindu society alive for the past eight hundred years.[2]

The exploration of the possibility of any positive response to Panikkar's cosmo-theandrism from the perspective of vedānta can be an evaluation of the success or failure of Panikkar's bridge-building between Catholicism and Hinduism.

The term, Vedānta, literally means the end of the Vedas. Although scholarship is not unanimous, and there is need of historical investigation of the different Vedas, especially by the Hindu scholars,[3] yet the present time scholarly consensus is: the earliest of the Vedas is the hymns of the Ṛg-Veda. These hymns are primarily concerned with sacrificial ritual although there are some speculations about the Absolute in them. Instructions and interpretations about the sacrificial rituals are laid down in the Yajur Veda and then in a body of literature written in prose called the Brāhmanas. The Brāhmanas seem to be concerned with how the sacrificer can be in rapport with the deity by meditating about the symbolic significance of the sacrifice. The Upaniṣads were attached to the Brāhmanas. Some early Upaniṣads deal with.the symbolic significance of the sacrifice, but they also speculated about the true nature of the Self. The "middle Upaniṣads" became contemptuous of the sacrifices and were concerned only with the true nature of self.

97

Perhaps sometimes before the Christian era
the exegists (Mimāmsakas) started to follow the
method of the other sciences to produce bodies of
aphorisms (sùtras) which could be easily memorized. The Sùtras were about the rules for the
interpretation of the Vedas and also cover their
main applications. The aphorisms in later period
were split into two separate bodies, known as the
Purva Mimāmsā Sùtras dealing with ritual and the
Uttara Mimāmsā Sùtras, also known as the Brahma
Sùtras, dealing with the realization of Brahman
or the Absolute. The exponents of Mimāmsā Sùtras
are known as the Mimāmsakas and those of the
Brahma Sùtras or Vedānta Sùtras as Brahma-Vādins
or Vedāntins. The term, Vedānta, now more
commonly means the different schools of thought
of Vedānta which are ten in number, each having
many sub-branches within it.[4] The different
Schools of Vedānta are directly related to the
Brahma Sùtras.[5] However, most of the Vedāntins
also showed their compatibility with the Mimāmsā
Sùtras. They taught how the Upanisadic teachings
of the realization of Self or the Absolute also
includes rituals. Gaudapāda, the forerunner of
Šamkara, and who is sometimes considered as the
first propounder of Advaita-Vedānta, advocated a
complete break from the Mimāmsā Sùtras and relied
completely on the Brahma Sùtras. Rituals are not
needed for liberation (Moksa).[6]

Of the ten Schools of Vedānta, Šamkara's
Kevalādvaita upholds the doctrine of uncompromi-
sing non-dualism. He is the exponent of the
jñāna yoga as the way to freedom as well as the
doctrine of māyā and avidyā. His school is
commonly designated as non-theistic and monistic
school of thought. All the other schools are
theistic. They recognize rituals together with
contemplation as means of salvation. Being
theists they are advocates of devotion. Rāmānuja
is one of the better known in whose theology the
characteristic of Theistic Vedānta is exemplified. Hence the two schools of Vedānta viz,
Šamakara's Kevalādvaita and Rāmānuja's
Višistādvaita can be considered as two represen-
tations of Hindu thought that can be noticed from
the time of the Vedas down to the modern period.
Therefore, most of the text books on Hinduism
deal mainly with these two schools of Vedānta.
We shall try to give a brief sketch of these two
schools to investigate whether and how far it is

possible to accept Panikkar's cosmo-theandrism from their perspectives.

It is very difficult to summarize Advaita and Viśistādvaita Vedānta as represented by Śaṁkara and Rāmānuja. The thoughts of these two masters have been variously interpreted by the successors of the schools. The interpretation of Sureśvarācārya (vārtikas and Naiskarmayasiddhi), Vācaspati (Bhāmatī), Padmapāda (Pancapādika) who were immediate successors of Saṁkara are different from each other. The interpretation of Sri Harsa (Khandanakhandakhādya) of the twelfth century is pure dialectic which may be further removed from Śaṁkara's intent and responsible for pure monistic interpretation of Śaṁkara. Even Yamunachārya who was forerunner of Rāmānuja distinguished Śaṁkara's idea from his later interpretations and used Śaṁkara's terminologies as kutastha to indicate the immutability of Brahman.[7] Therefore the difference between Śaṁkara's Vedānt and Viśistādvaita may not be as much as is usually considered. Again there were not only commentaries on Śaṁkara but commentaries on the commentaries. For example, Amālananda's Kalpataru (thirteenth century) is a commentary on Bhāmatī. Appayadiksita's Kalpataruparimāla (sixteenth century) is a treatise on Kalpataru.

In the case of Rāmānuja the interpretations of Sudarśana Bhatta (Srutaprakāsikā) Vedānta Deśika (Tattvartika and Tātparyacandrikā), Rangarāmāmuja (commentaries on Upanisads) in their differences may not be as radical as the different interpretations of Śaṁkara, yet the interpretations were colored by various concerns (e.g. Vedānta Desikā was fighting against the Tengali school with their indifference to the Sanskrit literature) and thus may not represent the true intent of Rāmānuja.

If we try to give our presentation of Śaṁkara and Rāmānuja on the basis of their own works the task is not any easier. Śaṁkara's works are enormous. He has commentaries on eleven Upanisads, Bhāgavad Gītā and Brahma Sūtra, besides Upadeśasahasri and Vivekacūdāmani which reflect his general position. The works of debatable authorship may not be taken into account. Again he composed many hymns to the different forms of the godhead, such as Daksināmūrti stotra, Ānandalahari, etc. To

reconcile the teachings of these works systematically is difficult and subject to differences of
opinion. That is why there are such diverse
interpretations of Śaṁkara. Rāmāmja's works are
not as many as Śaṁkara's. However, he attempted
the enormous task of reconciling the teachings of
the Upaniṣads, the Gitā, the Brahma Sūtras, the
Nārāyaniyā Section of Mahābhārata, Viṣṇu Purāna,
the Vaishnava Āgamas, and the works of the
Ālvāras and the Ācāryas. Therefore, any interpretation of Rāmāmuja also can be subject to
differences of opinion. Because of its wide
scope, Rāmāmuja's work could provide basis for
many movements in the subsequent history of
Hinduism. Radhakrishnan says, "The movements of
Madhva, Vallabha, Caitanya, Rāmānanda, Kabir and
Nānak, and the reform organizations of Brahmoism
are largely indebted to Rāmāmuja's theistic
idealism."[8] For the purpose of comparison with
Panikkar's theandrism we shall present Śaṁkara
and Rāmānuja's thoughts under the categories of
Brahman (God of Panikkar), Jiva (humans of
Panikkar), Jagat (world of Panikkar) and the
relationship among them.

Śaṁkara

Brahman

   Brahman, according to Śaṁkara, is the
ultimate reality. However, the term Brahman for
Śaṁkara is only a limiting concept for the
Ultimate which, according to him, is beyond all
ordinary means of human knowledge and beyond all
human categorizations. To say Brahman is reality
is only to indicate that it is different from the
phenomenal world. (Śaṁkara (S) Bhāsya (B);
IV.3.14). We may speak of it but we can neither
prove it by logic nor describe it. (S.B.iii, 2,
23). It is as the Upaniṣads say "...unseen,
beyond empirical dealings, beyond the grasp (of
the organs of action), uninferable, unthinkable,
indescribable"; (Mandukya up 7).[9] Therefore, it
is beyond any characterization (S.B.1. 3, 1).
That is why when Brahman is described in the
Srutis, it is mostly in negative terms. To
arrive at Brahman one has to go through neti
neti, not this, not this. Many critics think
(the western thinkers, such as Hegel, as well as
Indian thinkers such as Rāmānuja and the Nyāya
logicians) that if something is devoid of all
characterizations it amounts to pure non-entity.

Śaṁkara calls them Mandabuddi[10] or of inadequate
intelligence because they fail to see that even
totally imaginary things also have to have some
basis in reality.[11] Śaṁkara indicates that the
scriptures are the source of knowledge about
Brahman (S.B.1.1.3), and Amubhava (S.B.I,1,1) can
be the final assurance. However, even logic
indicates the need for an Absolute in the sense
of mind's inability to be contented only with the
relative.

In the scriptures in addition to the negative characterization of Brahman, there are some
positive descriptions. Śamkara indicates that
the conflicting scriptural statements can be
reconciled (S.B.I. 1. 1-31) by recognizing the
distinction between parā (ordinary) and aparā
(transcendent) knowledge. For the purpose of
conveying some initial ideas to people, positive
statements are used. Positive characters are
also for the purpose of worship. In Vedānta
philosophies a distinction is usually drawn
between the essential characteristics
(svarupalaksana) and the adventitious characteristics (tatastha laksana) of the Brahman. All
the Vedāntins think that Saccidānanda (existence,
consciousness, bliss) are Svarupalaksana.
However, Śaṁkara indicates that even this description also is only an approximation. Śaṁkara
does not want to have any compromise about the
ineffability of the Absolute.

Jiva

       According to Śaṁkara Jiva, or humans, in
essence is Ātman or self which is not different
from Brahman or the ultimate reality. In this
respect Jiva is coeval with time. Jiva is
neither born nor does it die. Birth and death
refers to the body only (S.B. 11, 3. 16-17),
which is an adjunct of the Ātman. Ātman is the
true transmigrator. Jiva, or the individual
human being, is Ātman with some invariable
physical adjunct[12] due to avidyā or ignorance.
Avidyā conceals (āvarana śakti) the real Ātman as
well as distorts it (vikhsepa śakti) and ascribes
to its qualities that do not really belong to it.
Although antahkarana or inner sense is physical
and hence unconscious, due to its closeness to
self it acquires a reflection of self (tadābhā)
thereby giving rise to the confusion caused by
non-discrimination between "I" and

101

"me"(Upadeśa-sahasri 18, 27). This
non-discrimination is responsible for ascribing
to the Ātman characteristics of agent (kartā),
enjoyer (bhoktā) and so on, which do not belong
to it. Ego-sense is an accompaniment of the Jiva
Thus according to Śamkara, Ātman with the adjunct
of avidyā is Jiva. Jiva in essence is Ātman.
That is why the Upaniṣada states, "That thou
art," tat tvam asi.

It is evident that according to Śamkara
Jiva, insofar as it is accompanied by the
ego-sense (ahamkāra), belongs to the realm of
"me," the object, and not "I," the subject. True
"I" can never be "me." There can ultimately be
only one true "I" and therefore, plurality
belongs to the realm of "me" or objects. Brahman
is the true "I." The individuals apart from
Brahman have no reality.
Jagat

Just as Jivas do not have any reality apart
from Brahman, so also the objects of the world
have no being apart from Brahman. The objects of
physical world are in time. They are the objects
of knowledge and as such are liable to destruction (yad drsyam tan nāsyam). Those objects,
which are objects of common knowledge, and the
objects of illusory perception, which are private, may differ in being relatively more permanent or less permanent, yet, both are
non-permanent. Both are canceled by more perfect
knowledge (Ātmabodha 6-17). The objects of
illusory perception as well as of common perception may be ultimately unreal (i.e., they are not
pāramārthika-ultimate), yet they have relative
reality--Prātibhāsika, or apparent, and
Vyāvahārika, or permanent, as long as worldly
consciousness is present. That is why Śamkara
calls the world as mithyā (phenomenon) rather
than asat (unreal). They are not mere mental
impressions. Śamkara denies the subjective
idealism (vijñāna vāda) or Śunyavāda which he
considers Nihilism (S.B. 2,2. 28-32). So long as
we have ego-sense the objects of the world are as
real as the individual living things. The
adhisthāna, or substratum of the illusory perception, is the real object behind it, e.g., when
the rope appears as a snake the rope is the real
substratum. Similarly, the substratum of the
perceptions of the world of objects in the waking
state is Brahman. Brahman is the reality. The

102

differences of names and forms are superimposed
on it by Màyà. The world is non-different from
(ananya), nonindependent (avyàtirikta) of
Brahman. (S.B. II. 1.14)
Relationship Between Brahman, Jiva and Jagat

It is evident from the above discussion that
according to Śaṁkara, Jiva and Jagat are totally
dependent on Brahman which is ultimate reality
underlying them. However, although they are
nothing apart from Brahman, they cannot either
singly or together stand for it. They are
phenomenal whereas Brahman is the reality. How
can they be related? "Na hi sadasatoh
sambandhs," there cannot be relationship between
the real and the unreal. Yet it is the real
which appears as the phenomenal and the ground of
the phenomenal is the real. According to Śaṁkara
the relationship between them is anirvacaniya,
indescribable. If Brahman is considered as the
cause of the phenomenal world then he can be
considered as efficient cause or as both material
and efficient cause. (Vedàntins do not talk
about formal and final cause in this context.) If
Brahman is only the efficient cause then there
has to be some material, over and above Brahman,
which is inadmissable. If Brahman is both the
efficient and the material cause, then it must go
through transformation, parināma, which cannot be
accepted for Brahman is immutable. Śaṁkara
therefore developed vivartavàda or the theory of
the apparent transformation of the cause into the
effect from the ajàtivàda of Gaudapàda (S.B. II,
1.14). If Brahman is considered the cause of the
phenomenal realm then it is not the immutable,
ineffable or nirguna Brahmana but Brahman with
the adjunct of màyà or saguna Brahmana or Iśvara.
Jivas can think of Him and adore and love Him.
When Brahman the ultimate reality is considered
in terms of the worldly realm then Iśvara, Jiva
and Jagat are the three chief elements which are
intimately related with each other. Brahman and
the worldly realm of Jiva and Jagat are not
identical for Brahman is not subject to the
mutations of the world. Brahman is real, the
world is phenomenal. Thus they are different.
Yet they are not different, non-dual, for the
basis of the world is Brahman. Only Brahman is
the ultimate reality. In that sense there is
only one reality. Plural reality is not
ultimate. Yet the plurality lasts as long as
worldly consciousness persists. Though the

plurality as such is not real, it is grounded in reality and denial of plurality is not the denial of reality. Therefore, on the one hand Šamkara admits the infinite difference between <u>Brahman</u> and the worldly realm, and on the other hand he says that they are not different. He uses the term non-different instead of identical in order to maintain the differences of the perspectives of <u>vyāvahārika</u>, or workaday, and <u>pāramārthika</u>, or transcendent. As long as we are on the ordinary level of consciousness the difference is significant, although from the transcendent perspective the unity is realized. Thus according to Šamkara <u>Brahman</u> is ineffable, apophatic. In relationship to <u>Jiva</u> and <u>Jagat</u> he is <u>Išvara</u>, the creator and the redeemer. <u>Jiva</u> in essence is <u>Brahman</u>, he is totally dependent on <u>Brahman</u>. <u>Jiva</u> with its ego-sense is different from <u>Brahman</u> and worships and adores Brahman. <u>Jagat</u> also is totally dependent on Brahman; it is not an illusion in the sense of human construct, but provides the ground for humans to realize their true nature.

Rāmānuja

<u>Brahman</u>

Rāmānuja, like Šamkara, believes that <u>Brahman</u> is the ultimate reality. However, for Rāmānuja <u>Brahman</u> is not a simple limiting concept. True, by our human endeavor we cannot know anything about Brahman. However:

> We know from the Scripture that there is a supreme Person whose nature is absolute bliss and goodness; who is fundamentally antagonistic to all evil; who is the cause of the origination, maintenance and dissolution of the world; who differs in nature from all other beings, who is all-knowing, who by his mere thought and will, accomplishes all his purposes; who is an ocean of kindness, as it were, for all those who depend on him, who is all-merciful; who is immeasurably raised above all possibility of anyone being equal or superior to him; whose name is the highest <u>Brahman</u>. (<u>Rāmānuja</u> (R) <u>Bhāsya</u> (B))[13]

Thus <u>Brahman</u> is not simply the cause of the world, he is also the supreme person with all the good qualities and devoid of all the evil ones (R.B. III. 2.11). He is absolute in the sense

104

that there is nothing which is equal to Him or
greater than Him. He is different from anything
of the world. He is also the God of love and
grace. The term Brahman is derived from the root
Brh, big or great.[14] It means that Brahman
possesses greatness of essential nature as well
as of qualities, is of ultimate fullness and as
such Lord of all (R.B.1.1.1). Rāmānuja does not
believe in vivartavāda and the causality ascribed
to Brahmana is parināma or real transformation
(R.B. 11.2.22). Brahman is both the efficient
and the material cause of the world (R.B. 11
4.20). Brahman is both the Viśesya, or referent,
of the qualities which are immutable and
viśesana, or the qualities which although changeable are real. Brahmana is the visesana, or the
changeable quality, only insofar as He is the
indwelling Ruler (antaryāmin) of all of them.
Thus he himself is not changeable. Changes and
imperfections belong to the worldly realm only.
Brahman is affected only in the sense that he is
the ruling principle, and hence the self of
matter and souls in their gross or evolved
states; but just because of that, i.e., his being
the inner ruler and self, he is not in any way
touched by the imperfections of the Viśesanas
(R.B. 1.4.27). Rāmānuja's Brahman is
cidācidaviśista, or qualified by Jiva and Jagat.
Individual souls and the world of objects emanate
from Brahman in the manner that the web emanates
from a spider-yathorna nābih srijate grhnateca.
Therefore saccidānanda is sarupalaksna or essential characteristic of Brahman. Brahman is
nirguna insofar as He does not have any imperfect
qualities. He is saguna as having all the
perfect qualities. There is no distinction
between the Iśvara or the Purusottama whom the
humans worship and the Brahman or the Absolute
who is the ground of all being (R.B.1.1. 20-21).

Jiva

According to Rāmānuja Jivas are individual
selves which are as real as Brahman although
totally dependent on Brahman. In his Gītā Bhāsya
11.12 he indicated the reality of the individual
souls and their distinction as well as dependence
on Brahman. According to Rāmānuja Jivas are
parts of Brahman as viśesanas or attributes of
Brahman. As parts of Brahman they are as real as
Brahman. "As the luminous body is of a nature
different from that of its light, so the Highest

105

Self (Brahman) differs from the individual soul
which is a part of it. As the attribute and the
substratum are not identical, the soul and
Brahman are not the same"[15] (R.B. 11.3.46). Jiva
being part of Brahman are dependent on Brahman.
However, God grants Jivas relative autonomy.
Rāmānuja's view is presented in terms of two
concepts: anumatidāna, or granting approval, and
dattvasātantra, or granted autonomy. "The
inwardly ruling highest self promotes action
insofar as it regards in the case of any action
the volitional effect made by the individual
soul, and then aids that effort by granting its
favor or permission (anumati). Action is not
possible without permission on the part of the
Highest Self" (R.B.11.3.41).[16] Thus the autonomy
of the individual is actually granted autonomy
(dattvasātantra). The individuals can turn away
from God. However, the God of grace also helps
them turn back towards Him (R.B.1.1.1). Rāmānuja
refers to Kathopanisad 11.23 to justify his view:
"The self cannot be attained by the study of the
Vedas, nor by intellect nor by such learning,
whom the self chooses by him it may be gained:
to him the self reveals itself."

Jivas in their essential nature are characterized by consciousness due to the presence of
the indwelling Ruler. The Upaniṣadic statement,
"tat tvam asi," or that thou art, does not refer
to the identity of Jiva and Braham but to the
fact that the one indwelling Ruler is present in
all the Jivas. The consciousness of the Jiva is
not vibhu or all pervasive as the consciousness
of the Brahman. It is subject to contraction and
expansion. In the condition of bondage it is
associated with gross body and the vital breath
which serve its purpose (R.B.11.4.10-11). Its
essential nature, then, remains hidden
(R.B.111.2.5). Until it becomes manifest the
soul goes from body to body but its essential
nature does not change. In the emancipated state
its essential nature is manifested and it remains
in a state of absolute bliss--
niratisayaakhandānubhava but as distinct from
Brahman.

Jagat

Like Jiva, Jagat also, according to
Rāmānuja, is as real as Brahman although also
totally dependent on Brahman. Jagat is the

unconscious part of Brahman. It constitutes the
objects of experience. They are subject to
change but that does not make them unreal. Jagat
constitutes the body of God through which He
reveals His glory. It does not constitute any
limitation for God as it might for humans. "To
the highest Brahman which is subject to itself
only, the same connection is the source of
playful sport, constituting in this, that He
guides and controls those things in various ways"
(R.B.111.2.12).17 The non-conscious entities of
the world work in obedience to God (R.B.11.2.2)
and provide the conditions for the realization of
the destinies of the Jivas. Thus jagat has two
functions. It reveals the glory of God and
provides the conditions for humans to reach their
goals of life.

Relationship Between Brahman, Jiva and Jagat

Like Śaṁkara, Rāmānuja believes in the
absolute dependence of Jiva and Jagat on Brahman.
However, Śaṁkara in his emphasis on the primacy
of Brahman does not consider Jiva and Jagat to be
as real as Brahman. Jiva and Jagat are mithyā if
not asat or unreal. For Rāmānuja Jiva and Jagat
are as real as Brahman. He recognizes a distinction of nature between non-sentient Jagat,
sentient Jiva and the ruling principle Brahman.
All are real although Jiva and Jagat are dependent on Brahman and Brahman is the controller of
Jiva and Jagat. He attempts to explain the
relationship between them in terms of several
analogies. Brahman is the cause of everything.
It goes through the modification of Jiva and
Jagat. The modified sentient and non-sentient
beings are not anything separate from Brahman.
They are parts of Brahman. Part here is not to
be understood in terms of extensions or of pieces
(khanda). They are parts of Brahman in the same
way as the lights issuing from a luminous body,
like fire or the sun, are parts of that body; or
the generic characteristics of a cow or a horse;
and black and white colored things, so colored,
are attributes and hence parts of things in which
these attributes inhere; or as the body is part
of all embodied beings. Brahman is the śariri,
or the soul, and Jiva and Jagat are śarira or
body. Brahman is the inner controller and ruler
of the world. Thus he is the King, and Jiva and
Jagat are the subjects. As the Bhāgavad Gitā
says, Brahman is the controller of the universe

107

as the one mounted on and running a
machine--Brahmāyam sarvabhutāni yantrādudani
māyayā. In the same way Brahman is the
Substance--(viśesya) and Jiva and Jagat are
attributes--(viśesanas). Sentient and
non-sentient beings are modes of the highest
Brahman and thus are real. He compares the
relationship between the three with a
three-colored piece of cloth where the thread of
each color remains ever distinct:

> Of some parti-coloured pieces of cloth the
> material cause is thread, white, red and
> black etc. All the same, each definite spot
> of cloth is connected with one colour only,
> white, e.g., and thus there is no confusion
> of colours even in the "effected" condition
> of the cloth. Analogously the combination of
> insentient matter, sentient beings, and the
> Lord constitutes the material cause of the
> world, but this does not imply any confusion
> of essential charectics of enjoying souls
> objects of enjoyment and the Universal Ruler
> even in the world s effected state. There is
> indeed a difference between the two cases,
> insofar as the threads are capable of exis-
> ting apart from one another and are only
> occasionally combined according to the
> volition of men while non-sentient matter and
> sentient beings in all their states form the
> body of the highest self and thus have a
> being only as modes of that..... But the two
> cases are analogous, in so far as there
> persists a distinction and absence of all
> confusion on the part of the constituent
> elements of the aggregate. This being thus,
> it follows that the highest Brahman although
> entering into the "effected" condition,
> remains unchanged, for its essential nature
> does not become different (R.B.1.1.1).[18]

Thus it seems that although Ramanuja emphasizes
the differences, the sameness is more important
and his view is therefore designated as qualified
non-dualism.

Śamkara, Rāmānuja and Panikkar

Śamkara's Kevalādvaita and Rāmānuja's
Visistādvaita have some obvious similarity.
According to both, humans and the world are
totally dependent on Brahman. They are nothing

apart from Brahman. But in order to maintain the ineffability of Brahman, Śaṁkara tends to give the plural world a doubtful status. In order to maintain the dignity and value of human adoration and aspiration for the divine, Rāmānuja tended to qualify that divine itself. Śaṁkara opened himself up to an abstract monistic interpretation although his intent might have been different as evidenced when he says, "to be born as human is one of the greatest boons that one can have." However, it is undeniable that in Śaṁkara the emphasis is on oneness, on non-difference rather than distinction, as is evident in his commentaries on Bṛhadāraṇyaka Upaniṣad (11.4.19), Chāndogya Upaniṣad (16), etc. The plurality belongs to the realm of nescience--only the false minded sees many and goes from birth to birth. By presenting the view of cidācidaviśiṣṭa Brahman, Rāmānuja opens himself up to a pantheistic interpretation of his philosophy, although his intent might have been different, as is evident from his repeated warning against considering the relationship between Brahman and Jiva-Jagat in spatial terms, in terms of parts put together. However, this is also undeniable that his notion of Brahman lacks the ineffability of Śaṁkara's notion. The problem of Śaṁkara and Rāmānuja is the problem of one and many--the problem of universality and concreteness.

According to Panikkar this is also the problem of Christianity. Christianity on the one hand is a historical, historically committed religion; on the other hand it is a universal religion, claiming to have a message for all humans, for all nations and all cultures. Panikkar proposes his cosmo-theandric view of reality to deal with the problem of Christianity as well as Hinduism. According to him both Christian and Hindu spirituality are theandric, non-dualistic, which is neither abstract unity nor unrelated plurality. Śaṁkara and Rāmānuja have a substantive way of thinking. Thus if they start with one substance they cannot explain the plurality, and if they start with many substances they cannot explain the unity. A similar difficulty can be noticed in Western Trinitarian thinking which started from the Nicene Creed. If there is one substance in the Trinity how can there be many persons or if there are many persons how can there be one substance? In a post-Einstein and post-Heideggar era in Western

109

Christian thinking, there is a tendency towards
relational and functional thinking as is evident
in Schoonenberg's Christological thinking. This
relational way of thinking is characteristic of
Buddhism, particularly the Mādhyamika School.
Panikkar, who is well acquainted with and well
versed in both Western thought and Buddhism,
proposed his cosmo-theandric view of reality,
which is relational and functional and not
substantive. God is one, ineffable, the true "I"
who has the "Thou" of the humans and the "It,"
"He," "She" as the ground of the "I"-"Thou"
relationship. According to Panikkar, God is not
the "thou" of the humans, but the other way
around. Like Śamkara he does not propose a
difference of degree of reality between God,
humans and world in order to maintain the absoluteness of God, nor does he compromise the
absoluteness of God to maintain the reality of
humans and world as Rāmānuja did. Like Śamkara
he says that God is one and ineffable, and like
Rāmānuja he says that the humans and the world
are also real. God is God, as one and ineffable,
but in relationship to humans and the world,
humans are real in relation to the ineffable God
and in relation to the concrete plurality of the
world; the world also is real in relationship to
God and the humans. They have different functions and exist in different relationships, but
not in different degrees.

It is apparent that from the perspective of
Rāmānuja's <u>Viśistā dvaita</u> Panikkar's cosmo-
theandrism is quite acceptable. Like Rāmānuja,
Panikkar emphasizes the three--God, humans and
the world--and indicates their differences.
Their differences do not imply their separate-
ness, but their underlying unity. It may seem
that from the perspective of Śamkara's uncompro-
mising absolutism, cosmo-theandrism is not
acceptable. However, like Śamkara, Panikkar says
that God is one and ineffable. He is the true
"I" and everything else is "me." The difference
between Panikkar and Śamkara seem to be that for
Śamkara the realm of "me" seems less significant
than the realm of "I." Yet as we have noted
before, Śamkara's intention was not to undermine
the importance of the worldly realm. He emphasized the fact that as long as the ego-sense
persists, God, humans and world are equally real.
We can say that Panikkar's cosmo-theandrism does
not violate the intention of either Rāmānuja or

Śaṁkara. All of them have similar concerns although they do not present their thought in the same way. None of them wants to compromise the oneness and unity of the ultimate reality. All of them believe there cannot be any reality apart from **Brahman** or God. .In other words all agree that the ultimate reality can be only one. However, none stops with the one; all also maintain that the one is the ground of the many. Śaṁkara says that the multiplicity is the apparent transformation of the one. Rāmānuja says that the multiplicity is the real transformation of the one. Panikkar says that the one is constituted by the multiplicity of relations.

Panikkar himself thinks that his cosmotheandric view of reality does not violate the intentions of Śaṁkara or Rāmānuja. This can be examined by presenting Panikkar's commentaries on some of the Hindu texts which are basis of Vedānta. Śaṁkara and Rāmānuja commented on those texts from the perspectives of their own views of reality. We shall first discuss Panikkar's commentary on **Brahma Sūtra** (1.1.2) which is concerned with the question of the relationship of world and **Brahman**. Then we shall discuss his commentaries on some of the **Mahāvākyas**[19] of the Upaniṣads which deal with the question of the relationship of humans and **Brahman**. The relationship between the world and the ultimate reality, or God, and the relationship between humans and God are the two issues regarding which Christianity and Vedānta are considered to be far apart. It is usually believed that in Hinduism particularly in Advaita Vedānta there is no idea of creation-the distinction between the creator and the creation and the difference between the creator and the creature is not maintained. Bede Griffiths, for example, says, "I would like to suggest that the critical question in regard to the relation of Vedānta to Christian faith is in this matter of creation."[20] Panikkar thinks that there is similarity of intention in both the traditions although doctrinally they are not presented in the same way.

Panikkar commented on Brahma Sūtra 1.1.2. **Janmādya asya yatah** in **The Unknown Christ of Hinduism**. We mentioned earlier that this is one of his earlier works, which appears to be more sectarian than his later works. Here, although the intuition of cosmo-theandrism is present, he

111

says that he is attempting a Christian <u>bhāsya</u> or
commentary of the Hindu text. He does not expect
the recognition of its authenticity from any
Hindu but appeals to a virgin mind. He believes
that he is not betraying the fundamental spirituality of Hinduism. Following the tradition of
the Hindu thinkers he analyzes the different
words of the Sutra and states that it means:
"That from which this origination, sustentation,
and transformation of this world, is Brahman."
<u>Brahman</u> thus may be considered as the cause of
the world. This, however, is problematic. How
can the immutable be the cause of the changeable?
We have discussed Śaṁkara's <u>Vivartavāda</u> and
Rāmānuja's <u>Parināmavāda</u>, the Christian thinkers
present the idea of creation <u>ex</u> <u>nihilo</u>. Each of
these involves philosophical problems. Panikkar
does not deal with the philosophical problem but
by commenting on the Sūtra he indicates how
mediation between the ineffable and changeable
takes place. <u>The</u> <u>Unknown</u> <u>Christ</u> <u>of</u> <u>Hinduism</u> was
originally Panikkar's Th.D. thesis. Naturally,
it has many details and complexities within it.
However, what he intends to say is simply stated,
the "that" referred to in the Sūtra is not
<u>Brahman</u> but <u>Iśvara</u>. The notion of <u>Iśvara</u> is not
completely identical with the notion of Logos.
However, the function of Logos, the Christ, is
similar to that of <u>Iśvara</u>. <u>Iśvara</u> is the mediator between the Absolute and the world. He is
the mediator not intermediary. Panikkar says:

Yatah, "from which," is one of the best names
of that supreme principle. This holds good
in a twofold direction. That "from which"
the world comes out is a genuine "whence,"
both in itself and as regards the world. Its
proper characteristic is to be a "from
which," an "originated" in a certain sense, a
"begotten," an "expression," an image. The
Logos is in itself the full Word, the total
manifestation of God the Father; it is really
God from God, Light from Light. That is to
say that even its proper "face" imaging the
Divinity is distinct from it, and yet there
is no lack of substantial identity, for Logos
has (<u>as</u> <u>receiver</u>) the whole divine nature
that the Father, Source of Divinity, has (<u>as</u>
<u>giver</u>). On the other hand, it is really
"that from which" the world comes out, it is
the Alpha and the Omega, that from which all

112

things take their being and in which all
subsist.[21]

We quoted Panikkar in detail to show the obvious
Christianness of his interpretation. He himself
is aware of it and calls it his Christological
Bhàsya. He himself says that his interpretation
cannot be found in any one of the Bhàsyakàras.
Nonetheless he feels that it was on the tip of
their tongue. When Panikkar was writing his
commentaries it seems that he had Śaṁkara Bhàsya
in mind. It is only in Śaṁkara that a distinction is made between the Nirguna Brahmana which
Panikkar compares to the notion of Father in
Christianity, and Sanguna Brahmana or Iśvara,
which Panikkar compares to the Logos or begotten
Son of Christianity.[22] From Śaṁkara's perspective
it is possible to agree with Panikkar's understanding of God, the Father (the apophatic aspect
of Godhead) and the Logos (the begotten Son
through whom everything is created). According
to Śaṁkara Brahman is not the creator, but Iśvara
is. Iśvara is Brahman with màyà. Both Iśvara
and the world are grounded in Brahman. But
Iśvara is creator and the world is created. Thus
perhaps from Śaṁkara's perspective it can be
admitted that Iśvara is begotten, world is
created and the ineffable ultimate reality is
related to the changeable world through Iśvara,
or in Panikkar's terminology Logos, although
these terms are quite foreign to Śaṁkara. In
reference to S.B.1v.14,19 f, perhaps it may be
indicated that in Śaṁkara, the Saguna and Nirguna
Brahman are distinguished and identified, just as
the Father and Son are identified and distinguished by Panikkar from his Christian perspective. It can also be noticed that the identity
of and difference between Saguna and Nirguna
Brahman are not like the identity and differences
of Panikkar's Father and Son. In Śaṁakara
identity is more important than difference.
Brahman with the adjunct of Màyà is Iśvara. The
distinction is true from the vyàvahàrika standpoint and not pàramàrthika. According to
Panikkar both identity and difference are important. The Son is the creative and mediating
aspect of Godhead--representing the real aspect
of the Godhead, the reality, adintra, which is
also reflected in reality, adextra. The economic
Trinity is the immanent Trinity and the immanent
Trinity is the economic Trinity. If from
Śaṁkara's perspective a response to this Chris-

tian terminology is to be made, it would be said that Śaṁkara would agree with Panikkar as far as the economic aspect of the Godhead is concerned, but he would refuse to say anything about the immanent aspect of the Godhead. According to him the immanent aspect of Godhead is the realm of transcendence and beyond human comprehension.

Rāmānuja does not distinguish between Saguna and nirguna Brahmana. He uses the term Brahmana and Īśvara interchangeably. He also identifies Brahman or Īśvara with Viṣṇu. In his commentary on Brahma Sūtra 1.1.2. he quotes a verse from Viṣṇu Purāna which states, "From Viṣṇu the world has sprung, in him it exists: "he is the cause of the subsistence and dissolution of the world and the world is he." Although Rāmānuja does not have different terms for God, the unoriginate, and god, the creator, for him both are real aspects of Godhead. From Rāmānuja's perspective the distinction between apophatic God and begotten creator is not meaningful. Panikkar's commentary on the Sūtra from Rāmānuja's perspective would seem to be too Śaṁkarite, who from Rāmānuja's perspective is a covert or cripto Buddhist! However, insofar as Panikkar admits the reality of distinctive aspects within the Godhead, Rāmānuja would agree with him. Rāmānuja would agree with Panikkar that the economic Trinity is the immanent Trinity and the immanent Trinity is the economic Trinity, although the terminology is foreign to Rāmānuja's way of thinking.

Panikkar commented on the mahāvākyas of the Upaniṣads, which deal with the question of the relationship of Brahman and ātman, in one of his recent works, The Vedic Experience. Here he says that the Upaniṣadic statement, ekam eva advitiyam, does not state only ekam, or one, but also states advitiyam, or not-two. It should not be interpreted as either monism or dualism. Panikkar says that the ultimate object of human experience is one. "This One, this ekam, is qualified in a very special way. It is in fact the qualifying word, advitiya, which renders the affirmation of oneness fruitful and rescues it from being a barren tautology."[23] The clue to this advitiya, or oneness, and plurality can be found in consciousness. Consciousness can have plurality of objects of consciousness without losing its unity. That is why it is said,

Prajñānan Brahman (consciousness is Brahman).
Everything is the object of consciousness. But
consciousness by definition cannot be the object
of consciousness. The Upaniṣads give the direction about the order that we should follow to
discover consciousness. We are not to seek the
objects but should try to discover the subject.
However, the subject cannot be treated as object.

Thus we arrive at the fundamental paradox of
consciousness: its purity is destroyed by
self-consciousness. Pure consciousness
cannot be dualistic, but advaitic knowledge
is really ineffable. Consciousness is not
VAC, the word, but that which permits the
word to be.[24]

Panikkar's explanation of the statement,
Ātman is Brahman, which indicates the relationship between individual selves and the Supreme,
is ingenious in indicating non-duality, neither
identity (ekatva) nor duality (dvaitva) between
the two. Usually Vedāntic or Śaṁkar's spirituality is condemned for destroying all distinctions between the individual self and God. It
contains statements such as, the salt (individual
self) gets dissolved in the water (supreme self)
and "the drops of waters (selves) merge in the
totality of the ocean (God)." Panikkar interprets
these two analogies to justify his thesis that
individuality is opposed to plurality but not to
personality.[25]

In dealing with the example of salt and
water, he says, that the salt being dissolved in
water only loses its form (individuality) but not
its saltness (personality). We are tempted to
quote him in detail:

The salt dissolved in the pond of water has
not ceased to be salt because it has lost its
form and perhaps also its name as a separate
entity called salt. It becomes more truly
itself in fulfilling its mission of making
things salty than it would if it had remained
as a mere lump. The salt in the ocean is, in
a way, more truly salt than the isolated
lump, just as money is more truly money when
fruitfully circulating than when frozen in a
private safe.[26]

Panikkar wants to hold a functional and relational view of personality and not substantive. This was noticed in connection with his Christology also.[27]

Panikkar's treatment of the example of the drop of water and the ocean also is very interesting. The drop of water does not lose its personality in being merged in the ocean. Panikkar makes a distinction between the drop of water and the water of the drop. In the former the emphasis is on the water and the external tension is only adventitious. The individual drop of water would be lost in merging with the ocean. In the second case the emphasis is on the speciality of the water of the drop. When the surface tension disappears the peculiarity of the drop of water does not disappear. Rather its function as water, now being free from all limitations, becomes more fulfilled.

If we accept that the individuality is the surface tension and personality the water of the particular drop, we may agree in saying that when the human being dies, his individuality disappears while his personality remains and even enhanced. For what until then were only external relations across the barriers of finiteness have now become internal relationships.[28]

Panikkar wants to say that the concern of Hindu spirituality is to emphasize both identity of and differences between individual selves and ultimate reality. In the presentation of Śaṁkara and Rāmānuja, this was noted to be so.

The similarity of the concerns of Śaṁkara, Rāmānuja and Panikkar and the differences of their ways of dealing with them can be indicated clearly by comparing their commentaries on the mahāvākya, "tat tvam asi" (that thou art), which the Hindus consider the most important mahāvākya. This was the cornerstone of Śaṁkara's Vedānta. Rāmānuja indicated the limitation of Śaṁkara's explanation and interpreted the mahāvākya from the perspective of Viśistādvaita. Panikkar comments on the mahāvākya from the perspective of cosmo-theandrism which he thinks does not violate the intentions of Śaṁkara or Rāmānuja. Śaṁkara commented on this mahāvākya, statement in his commentary on Chandogya Upaniṣad. He explained

116

this in Brahma Sùtra Bhàsya as well as Upadeśa
sahasri. His commentary emphasized the
non-difference of the essence of Jiva and
Brahman. "Tat," according to Śaṁkara refers to
Nirguna Brahmana, or the Brahman that cannot be
characterized by any qualities. "Tvam" refers to
the essence of Jiva, not the Jiva with the
ego-sense due to ignorance but to àtman which is
not different from Brahman. Śaṁkara emphasizes
all the identity statements of the Upaniṣadas and
explains those which describe the Jivàtmà as
different from or as parts of paràmatmà (ultimate
reality) as being statements which refer to the
vyàvahàrika standpoint in order to facilitate
adoration and worship. Jiva or the humans from
the empirical perspective are different from
Brahman, but the essence or the ultimate nature
is identical with Brahman. Ràmànuja considers
Śaṁkara's explanation one-sided. He thinks that
Śaṁkara is not giving enough credit to human
adoration and worship. He explains "tat" as
referring to Brahman. Brahman, according to
Ràmànuja, is not an abstract unity but contains
concrete distinctions. "Tvam," according to
Ràmànuja, refers to the Brahman that is present
in every human being as an indwelling
Lord-antaryàmin. The indwelling Lord and the
Ultimate Reality which is Brahman are of course
the same. But the jivàtmà and the paramàtmà are
not identical. Jivàtmà, or the individual soul,
resides in a physical body and its consciousness
is subject to contraction and expansion. It is
never all pervasive like Brahman. Paramàtmà
resides in the jivàtmà, which is its body and
through it also resides in the physical body.
The causal Brahman is identical to the Brahman
immanent in effect, but Brahman, the cause, is
not identical with the effect--the jiva and
jagat. Ràmànuja indicates that the identity
statements of the Upaniṣads refer to the fact
that the same transcendent Brahman is immanent in
the individual souls but is not thereby exhaus-
ted. Therefore there are the statements of
differences also.

According to Panikkar this mahàvakya is the
true explication of ekam eva advitiyama. This
statement like the other mahàvakyas shows the
non-duality of reality. However, this mahàvkya
is special in its existential import. It indicates how we can find our true selves in our
relatedness to the Brahman. Panikkar thinks that

117

this statement indicates the personal or relational characteristic of reality to show that it
is neither "one" nor "two." It is non-dual. (In
this context Panikkar discusses the distinction
between individuality and personality as he does
in the context of his Christology.) Persons are
unique and beyond numerical characterization
because they are constituted by relationship.
Personal relationships cannot be repeated. The
individual personalities of "I" (first person),
thou (second person), heúsheúit (third person)
are formed by their relationships with each
other.[29] Brahman is the "I" (tat) which implies
the "thou" (tvam). Śvetaketu (human being) is
the "thou" of Brahman, nothing more, nothing
less. Nothing more, because without Brahman he
has no being--he is nothing. Nothing less
because he is equal to Brahman having infinite
value as the "thou" of Brahman. Diverging from
the usual Judaeo-Christian expressions, Panikkar
says that God is "One" not "other," God is "I"
not "thou." Panikkar admits that Brahman is the
Absolute. However, there is an aham (literally
"I" but Panikkar means the second person) and an
ayam, a sa, a tad, a he (i.e., the third person).
He says that if Upanisads only wanted to show the
identity of àtman and Brahman the statement could
be tvam tat asi (thou art that). However, the
Upanisad states tat tvam asi (that thou art). It
implies discovery to find out our "thou" characteristic, i.e., our dependence on God as well as
our freedom in response to God.

Panikkar indicates that the very form in
which Uddyalaka instructs Śvetaketu in the
Chhàndogya Upanisad also proves his thesis.
Uddyàlaka instructed Śvetaketu nine times. Each
time the sat (existence) aspect of the creatures
is emphasized. "All creatures, my friends, have
sat as their root, have sat as their abode, have
sat as their support (ground,pratistha)."[30] Each
time the instruction concludes with the statement, "That which (is) this ultimate element, all
this (world) has as its self, that is reality,
that is àtman, that art thou, Śvetaketu."[31]
Panikkar says that, "there is a significant
change of person from the original elliptic third
person of the verb to be to the second person in
the last part of the sentence--from the asti to
asi."[32] Everything of the world is grounded in
Brahman. So is Śvetaketu. Yet he (the human
person) is not an indiscriminate part of the

universe. He is the partner of Brahman, neither
separated nor unrelated but his "thou," his other
pole, his tension, his 'person,' as we might
cautiously add."[33] Panikkar thinks that "personhood" is a better characterization of humans
rather than God. God is person only as the "I"
of the "thou" (humans). Our ordinary human
experience shows that the consciousness of
"personhood" develops from the "thou-conscious-
ness" and not from "I-consciousness." We become
conscious of "personhood" by being aware of our
being loved, cared for or sought by others or in
an opposite by being despised, neglected, etc.
There is only one true "I" Brahman. (Human
beings are "thou" of Brahman and the true
"I-thou" relationship also implies a
"he/she/it.") Panikkar interprets tat tvam asi in
the light of his theandric intuition. He indicates that the relationship between human persons
and the Ultimate is neither identity nor difference. Again, the relationship between the
humans and the ultimate is not identical to the
relationship between world and the ultimate, nor
is it totally different.

      Certain similarities as well as differences
between Śaṁkara, Rāmānuja and Panikkar can be
pointed out. All agree in the absoluteness of
the Ultimate. All agree that human beings are
totally dependent on Brahman. Panikkar agrees
with Śaṁkara in maintaining that the true "I" is
the Brahman. He agrees with Rāmānuja in maintaining that human beings also are equally
important. However, there are also differences.
Whatever may be the intuition of Śaṁkara, in
explaining tat tvam asi he compares it with the
statement "this is Devadatta," and ultimately
reduces it into a tautological statement.
Rāmānuja rightly criticizes Śaṁkara by indicating
that if the statement were a mere tautology it
would not be significant, and Panikkar would
agree. However, if there are two how can their
non-difference be indicated? Rāmānuja's explanation of Samānādhikaranya (being in the same
substratum) does not resolve the problem.
Śaṁkara and Rāmānuja are conscious of the problem
of identity and difference. Śaṁkara, therefore,
devises the technical notion of tādātmya (identity of essence) and Rāmānuja aprithak Siddhi
(notseparateness) to handle the situation.
Compared to Śaṁkara and Rāmānuja, Panikkar's
presentation seems to be strikingly ingenious.

He is equipped with the modern method of linguistic analysis. He can show the difference between asti (is) and asi (are) to specify the relationship between Brahman and human beings. The difference between Śaṁkara and Rāmānuja on the one hand and Panikkar on the other is the difference of their ways of thinking. Śaṁkara and Rāmānuja both think in substantive terms. This is atomistic, and therefore relation becomes a difficult problem. Panikkar on the other hand thinks in relational terms. This is nonatomistic, and the problem of relation is obviated. Śaṁkara and Rāmānuja both state that "tat" and "tvam" both ultimately refer to Brahman. If "tvam" refers to the individual souls with its limitations and imperfections then there cannot be any identity between Brahman and Ātman. According to Śamkara, "tvam" refers to the essence of the individual soul which is only a reflection of the true essence of Brahman. He emphasizes Brahma Sūtra 2.3.50 and explains multiplicity as apparent—abhāsa eva ca . Rāmānuja things that "tvam" refers to the Brahman who is really immanent in multiple human beings. Panikkar says that "tvam" refers to the human beings as the "other" of "tat" or Godhead. According to him God is the God of human beings and human beings are so because of God. Their relationship cannot be explained in terms of identity or difference. Panikkar is not violating the intentions of Śaṁkara and Rāmānuja. He is indicating that the "thou" is totally dependent on the "that" and yet it is equally important as the "thou" of the "that." Rāmānuja would readily agree. In Śaṁkara the "thou" seems to be less significant than the "that." However, it has to be indicated that according to Śaṁkara as long as we are in vyāvahārika, or the worldly realm, in order to be able to realize the pāramārthika or the ultimate we have to equally emphasize the I, thou, he/she/it. This is quite evident in his statements regarding spiritual qualifications for Brahma jijñāsa or the quest of Brahman (S.B.1.1.1).

Our analysis of Śaṁkara, Rāmānuja and Panikkar indicates that it is possible to have a bridge between Catholicism and Vedāntic Hinduism in both of its important forms if Catholicism and Vedānta both are interpreted in terms of Panikkar's cosmo-theandrism. In chapter three we have indicated that cosmo-theandrism is not

120

foreign to Catholic spirituality. Our analysis of Śaṁkara and Rāmānuja shows that it is also congenial to Vedāntic spirituality. However, Catholicism as a tradition with its dogmas and doctrines about Christ, Trinity, Church, etc. as they are developed through the Christian centuries, is more than cosmo-theandrism. Similarly, Vedānta with its world view, with its doctrines about <u>Brahman</u> <u>ātman</u>, etc., as are developed throughout the history of Hinduism, also is more than cosmo-theandrism. The specifics of each tradition are grounded historically and are difficult to fit into another tradition. It is, therefore, evident that bridge building is possible on some universal perspective which can serve as the common ground between the two traditions. The specifics would be on the two sides of the bridge. The specifics of each tradition are to be reinterpreted in the light of the common ground, as Panikkar did in his interpretations of Christian doctrines and also of some Hindu texts. This enables a communication between the two traditions if not also a communion.

Notes

Vedānta and Panikkar

[1] Radhakrishnan, Indian Philosophy (George Allen-Urvin, Reprint, 1948), vol. 2, p. 430.

[2] Śivānanda, Bliss Divine (The Yoga Vedanta Forest Academy, 1964),p. 498.

[3] From the Hindu perspective history is de-emphasized as ultimate Truth is transtemporal. However, the Hindus also believe that the trans-temporal Truth is variously expressed in the temporal and thus history is not unimportant. At least from the perspective of scholarship there is need for historical studies of the texts to investigate the truth of the Hindu claim, e.g., by Aurobindo, that the Vedas are not chronological and that the chronological arrangement of the Vedas by Western Scholars, e.g., Oldenberg, should be rejected.

[4] The term which now more commonly means the different schools of Vedāntic thought, represents ten schools of Vedanta, each of which has many branches as sub-systems. 1) Kevalādvaita or Absolute non-dualism of Śamkara, 2) Viśistādvaita or qualified non-dualism of Rāmānuja, 3) Bhedāvada or doctrine difference (dualism) of Madhva, 4) Sābhāvikā dvaitādvita or Natural-dualism-non-dualism of Nimbārka, 5) Suddhādvaita or Pure non-dualism of Vallabha, 6) Aupādhika-bhedābheda Vāda or doctrine of adventitious difference-non-difference of Bhāskara, 7) Visistā sivā dvaita or doctrine of qualified non-dualism with Sivā of Śrikantha, 8) Suddhādvaita or Pure non-dualism of Visnusvāmim, 9) Viśesadvaita or special non-dualism 'of Śripati, 10) Acintya Bhedāveda or inexplicable difference.

[5] The Brahma Sūtra of Bādarāyana is the one commented upon by the different schools. How-ever, his work itself shows that there were at least seven other Vedāntic teachers.

[6] In tracing the development of the Vedāntic Schools from the Vedas primarily the introduction in the book of A. J. Alston, "That

Thou Art" (Shanti Sadan, 29 Chapston Villas,
London W 11, 1967) is
followed.

7 W. G. Neevel, Jr., in Yāmuna's Vedanta
and Pañcarātra, indicated in similarity of Yamunā
and Šamkara.

8 Radhakrishnan, Indian Philosophy, vol. 2
(reprint, ed., George Allen and Unvin, 1948), p.
670.

9 Eight Upanisads, trans. by Swāmi
Gambhirānanda, 2nd ed. (Calcutta: Advaita
Ashrama, 1966), vol. 2, p. 206.

10 S.B., Chāndogya Upanisad, viii, 1.1.

11 "Sunyam eva tarhi tat, na,
mithyāvikalpasya nirnimittvānupapatteh." There
cannot be a pure void because even false desires
would not leave meaning if it were so. (S.B. on
Gaudapāda's Karika)

12 According to Hindu philosophies the
physical adjuncts need not necessarily be the
gross physical body which can be known through
the external sense organs, but can be the subtle
body like antahkarna (the inner organs, compri-
sing manas or mind, buddhi or intellect or
determinate faculty, Chitta or pleasure-seeking
function, and ahamkara or ego-sense).

13 Radhakrishnan, Brahma Sūtra (London:
George Allen and Unwin Ltd., 1960), p. 563.

14 The etymological meaning of Brahman is
that which grows. See Gonda, Notes on Brahman
(Utrecht: 1950).

15 Radhakrishnan, Brahman Sūtra, p. 418.

16 Yamunācārya, Rāmānuja's Teachings in His
Own Words, (Bombay: Bhanatiya Vidya Bhavan,
1963), p. 104.

17 Radhakrishnan, Brahma Sūtra, p. 451.

18 M. Yamunācārya, Rāmānuja's Teachings, pp.
79-80.

123

[19] The four sayings of the Upanisads are as follows: "Ekam eva advitiyam," "Aham Brahnasmi," "Ayamātma Brahmā," "Tat tvam asi."

[20] Bede Griffiths, Vedānta and the Christian Faith, p. 43.

[21] Panikkar, The Unknown Christ of Hinduism, pp. 127-128.

[22] Śamkara Bhāsya states that the Supreme Lord abides in two forms, the transcendental and the empirical.

[23] Panikkar, The Vedic Experience, p. 656.

[24] Ibid., p. 688.

[25] See chap. III.

[26] Panikkar, The Vedic Experience, p. 700.

[27] See chap. III.

[28] Panikkar, The Vedic Experience, p. 701.

[29] Hence we may note the similarity of Panikkar's thinking with Schoonenberg. Schoonenberg indicates that the three persons of the Trinity should be understood in relational terms and not in a substantive way. See The Christ (New York: Seabury Press, 1971).

[30] Panikkar, The Vedic Experience, p. 751.

[31] Ibid., p. 751.

[32] Ibid., p. 751.

[33] Ibid., p. 752.

CONCLUSION

Our discussion on Panikkar's dialogue with Hinduism as a communication or bridge between Hinduism and Catholicism indicates that it is viable. However, if we try to estimate the success of this bridge building in terms of the actual responses of the Hindus and the Catholics, the conclusion would not be as categorical. We have mentioned in the introduction that we did not encounter any written comment on Panikkar by any Hindu thinker. There may be various reasons for it. Panikkar writes in various Western languages and not only in English. Most of the Hindu thinkers are not acquainted with the languages in which Panikkar writes. Again, Panikkar writes primarily for the Christians. This is in accordance with his general stance that dialogue is primarily for learning. He attempts to integrate the Hindu experience with Christian spirituality. Although if this integrated view is accepted by both the partners of dialogue it is the ideal, his concern nonetheless seems more to be acceptable to the Catholics than to the Hindus. Most Hindus are not aware of Panikkar, and the few that know of him are not acquainted with his thought in depth. My discussion with some Hindu scholars and religionists has made this very evident to me. They did not deal with the questions of whether Panikkar's understanding of Hinduism is authentic, whether Panikkar's interpretation of Christianity is more congenial from the perspectives of Hinduism. They expressed their unhappiness by pointing out that he is still a Christian and makes universal claims for Christianity. These Hindus who are so proud of their tolerance should, in order to be consistent with their principle, rather be happy that Panikkar remains faithful to his <u>sva-dharma</u>, his own <u>dharma</u> and does not opt for <u>paradharma</u> or other's <u>dharma</u>, which according to the teachings of the Bhāgavad Gitā is of grave consequence.[1] These Hindu thinkers, however, do not express their unhappiness with Panikkar in terms of his remaining a Christian, but rather in terms of his universal claim for Christianity. They fail thereby to see that in order to be true to his Christian faith he has to make this universal claim, just as the Hindus, in order to be true to their faith, have to advocate plurality. In

actuality Panikkar is not any less tolerant than
the Hindu thinkers and the Hindu thinkers are not
any less exclusivistic than Panikkar. The
problem is the problem of two absolute truth
claims. Panikkar's proposed model of dialogue is
to understand these absolute truth claims, and to
attempt to integrate each other's experience to
establish communication with each other instead
of remaining in one's own closed system.

Hindus in general are not aware of
Panikkar's model of dialogue. They are suspi-
cious, and not without reason, that dialogue is
another trick on the part of Christians to
convert them. We shall quote a Hindu, Sivendra
Prakash, who declined to participate in dialogue
with the Christians in 1970 to indicate the
general Hindu attitude:

> Of course it would be delightful for
> me...to share some at least of our best
> experience in our common endeavour towards
> the divine goal. Yet, to be quite frank with
> you, there is something which makes me uneasy
> in the way in which you Christians are trying
> so eagerly now to enter into official and
> formal dialogue.
>
> Have you forgotten that what you call
> the 'inter-faith-dialogue' is quite a new
> feature in your understanding and practicing
> Christianity? Until a few years ago--and
> often today still--your relations with us
> were confined either to a merely social plane
> or to preaching in order to convert us to
> your dharma.... You should not be surprised
> therefore, when not a few among us suspect
> your 'stretched-out hand' and your sweet
> invitation for dialogue....
>
> I am afraid really that when you call us
> to dialogue you do not understand spiritual
> dialogue in the way we do. You want infor-
> mation; you want learned discussion on
> phenomenal aspects of religion.... All are
> things of human interest, I do not deny it,
> but all remains short of the ultimate--the
> parama pada--which alone interests the man
> who got even a glimpse of the inner
> Mystery....

Do you understand now that the dialogue
you aim at is terribly limited in scope? It
is possible only at the level of University
professors on both sides--something like a
symposium on comparative religion. Some will
probably be interested in it, but excuse me,
I am not. I long for the only dialogue which
ill help one to realize more deeply the
Mystery of the Spirit in me.[2]

Prakash's reluctance indicates that the psychological condition for dialogue is dialogue on equal
terms. If anyone is convinced that s/he knows
what the ultimate truth is, s/he cannot have a
partner in dialogue. S/he would also be inca-
pable of dialogue. S/he can engage in debate or
monologue but not dialogue. Panikkar's model is
psychologically the best possible one and Prakash
would not be reluctant in such dialogue. Klostermaier also is advocate of dialogue on equal
terms. The scholars who are deeply involved in
inter-religious dialogue recognize this fact.
This is evident in Leonard Swidler's editorial
note in the Journal of Ecumenical Studies.[3]
Dialogue needs honesty and the recognition of
honesty of the partners of dialogue. Thus,
although the actual responses to Panikkar by
Hindus may be scarce and negative, yet insofar as
he is advocating and also pursuing his dialogue
with Hinduism with some success, as we have
indicated in our discussion, he is removing the
barrier to Hindu-Christian dialogue.

Panikkar indicates that to be engaged in
dialogue a self-critical attitude is a prerequi-
site. Among the Hindus in general there seems to
be a lack of self-criticism. In the writings of
the prominent Hindu thinkers we encounter apolo-
getics (Radhakrishnan), a militant attitude
(Vivekānanda), and complacence (Nikhilānanda and
many other monks of Ramakrishna order). It is
not that they are not critical of anything in the
Hinduism of their time. Rather, all of them
advocate reform of Hinduism. However, in general
the diagnosis as well as the remedy is thought of
in terms of the ancient and there is hardly any
attempt to reinterpret the old in terms of the
new. This is also true of Gandhi. In order to
establish Rāma Rājya he wanted to turn the wheel
of time back to past and that is impossible. The
cause of the problems of Hinduism was and is
still considered by most of Hindu thinkers to be

a falling from the ideal of Hinduism. If there is any problem in the ideal itself or at least in the presentation of the ideal and how it can be achieved, it is not explored by most of them.

The reasons for this lack of a self-critical spirit among the Hindu thinkers are very complex. Feeling of national pride, the richness and boldness of the different Hindu philosophical traditions, the varieties and flexibilitas within Hinduism, all are contributing factors. The criticism of Hinduism by the West in general and Christian missionaries in particular also was not helpful in stimulating self-reflection. Although the first reaction to criticism by outsiders is defensive, if the criticisms are cogent it can ultimately lead to analysis. The different Hindu thinkers' criticism of a too narrow understanding of Christ and Christianity stimulated Christian thinking. The usual criticism of Hinduism by the West as other-worldly, illusionistic, unethical, etc., could be easily refuted by the Hindu thinkers for its factual incorrectness.

Panikkar's criticism of Hinduism, however, is not on a superficial level. His diagnosis of the problem of Hinduism is the separation of the universal from the concrete. The Hindu philoso- phers have developed subtle intellectual systems. They have emphasized the universal aspects of truth. How the universal is related to the concrete pluralities of the world remains a problem. This we have noted in chapter V in connection with Šamkara and Rāmānuja, the two chief exponents of the two most important schools of Hindu thought. The discussion of the rela- tionship of the universal and particular is one of the important topics of the different philo- sophical schools of Hinduism. Panikkar's criti- cism should make the Hindus self-conscious and stir them to probe into the problems of Hinduism. This would stimulate reinterpretation and a new understanding of the doctrines of Hinduism, and thus also lead Hindus to dialogue with Catholics.

Panikkar's impact on the Christians is more evident than on the Hindus, both positively and negatively. Any Christian thinker who is in- volved in dialogue with Hinduism knows and responds to Panikkar. There is hardly any book on Hindu-Christian dialogue written by the Christian authors in contemporary time that does not refer to Panikkar. The Christian thinkers in general are appreciative of Panikkar's universalistic and integral interpretation of Christianity. All the articles written about Panikkar would justify this contention.[4] However, most of his Christian critics are unhappy about what they consider his minimizing of Jesus of Nazareth. Panikkar is not willing to identify Christ with Jesus of Nazareth. He says, "When I call this link between the finite and the infinite by the name Christ, I am not presupposing its identification with Jesus of Nazareth. Even from right within the Christian faith such an identification has never been made."[5] In chapter III we have seen how Panikkar attempts to justify himself from within the Christian tradition. However, it is equally true that even today there are many Christians who do make this identification. Panikkar would claim that this is emphasizing the concrete at the expense of the universal and it may amount to idolatry. Panikkar's criticism is worth pondering and there are thinkers who consider the problem. Panikkar's dialogue with Hinduism may not have generated many Hindu responses yet, and all Catholic thinkers may not agree with him, yet insofar he has removed the barriers of dialogue from the Hindus and stimulated the Catholic thinkers, he has been successful in establishing some connections between Hindus and Catholics. He has demonstrated that bridge building between two traditions upholding two absolute truth claims is a possibility.

In chapter I we discussed Panikkar's proposed scheme of inter-religious dialogue. We noted its advantages as well as its problems. From his actual dialogue with Hinduism we may note some further points about inter-religious dialogue. Panikkar's dialogue suggests that there may be one absolute Truth but the intellectual formulations about that absolute truth can be various because of the human factors involved, as well as because of the transcendence of the Truth. Different religious traditions which offer different doctrines about the transcendent Truth can, therefore, learn from each other. This learning takes place not by putting the different doctrines side by side or by addition of one to the other. Rather, this learning occurs by deepening the insights of one's own tradition in light of the other. For example, in dialogue with Hinduism the Christian is not

simply to put the Vedāntic experience beside the
Christian experience, nor to add it up with
Christian experience but to attain a deeper
insight into Christ. In the same way a Vedāntin
is not to put the experience of Christ besides
his experience or add it up with his own, but to
deepen his insight about that vedāntic experience
itself.

   Panikkar's dialogue with Hinduism indicates
the advantages of the relational world view
rather than a substantive one for the purpose of
dialogue. Substantive world views are atomistic
and exclusivistic. Accommodation of plurality
within this framework is difficult. We have
noted this in chapter V. Both Christianity and
Vedānta interpreted in substantive terms may seem
exclusivistic of each other. On the other hand,
a relational world view interprets reality in
terms of a network of relationships; no point in
this network is separated and separable from the
others. Plurality can be accepted and relativity
indicated without admitting absolute relativism.
There is room to learn from each other without
giving up the distinctiveness in the common
pursuit of the ultimate Truth.

   Again, Panikkar's dialogue indicates that in
order to profit from each other the partners in
dialogue must probe into the intent of each
other's doctrines and should not stop at mere
intellectual understanding of the different
doctrinal formulations. Panikkar indicates that
the intent of non-dualism of Hinduism is to
advocate identity as well as difference between
the divine and the worldly. In the same way the
intent of the Trinitarian doctrine of Christianity is to uphold the difference as well as
identity of the three persons. Understanding of
the intellectual formulations and linguistic
analysis are helpful insofar as they can reveal
the true intent of the doctrines. In other words
Panikkar is advocating dialogue in depth.

   Panikkar's integrated interpretation of
Christianity is subject to some criticism from
the point of view of internal consistency. His
main concern is to hold together universality and
concreteness. With this end in mind he distinguishes between historical and transhistorical
Christianity, Jesus and Christ, visible Church
and Mystical Body, while at the same time holding

on to their inseparability. In each case the
actual relationship between the historical and
trans-historical remains rather vague and unspe-
cified. His distinction between Christianity as
Super Religion and historical Christianity is
interesting. Following his own logic he has to
assign to historical Christianity the same status
as other traditions of the world. In his earlier
works he was reluctant to do so. In his later
works although he explicitly states that insofar
as historical Christianity is social it is
similar to the other traditions, yet he claims
that the Super Religion is more concretely
manifested in historical Christianity than in any
other traditions; Christ is manifest in Christianity but only hidden in other religions. Why
that is so, he does not specify. In the same way
he identifies Christ with the universal mediating
principle between the divine and the worldly and
not to Jesus of Nazareth, but he says that this
principle has a sui generis relationship with
Jesus of Nazareth. Even though everything is
Christophany, Christ is fully manifested in Jesus
of Nazareth. Again he does not explain how and
why? The problem of the visible Church and
Mystical Body is similar and his treatment of
this specific problem is very ingenious. He
indicates that the concrete expression of the
Mystical Body in the visible Church has the
possibility of an ever widening horizon because
the visibility does not depend only on the object
perceived but on the perceiver as well. People
may not only have limited vision in the sense of
having narrow range of vision, they may even
suffer from myopia!

Panikkar's Trinitarianism or what he prefers
to call cosmo-theandrism seems to be intellectually the most unclear and problematic. He
calls it a vision or intuition. The way he
explicates it leaves many questions unanswered.
The interrelatedness of the divine-human-cosmic
can be understood, but the relatedness of this ad
extra to the ad intra remains vague. Like
Rahner, Panikkar indicates that the economic
Trinity is the transcendent Trinity and vice
versa. But how that is so neither of them can
explicate quite clearly. Some critics of
Panikkar condemn him as Christo-pantheist.[6]
Panikkar says that the ultimate reality is one in
the sense that everything is dependent on God and
hence there cannot be anything other than God.

Creation is totally dependent on God--it is
nothing without God. Yet the creation is for
God, of God and in God, and thus different from
God. Panikkar omits only the pantheistic statement that the world is God!

In fairness to Panikkar, however, it should
be noted that he does not claim that he has
solved all the intellectual problems of universality and concreteness, that he has deciphered
the Ultimate Mystery. He believes in growth and
development. He offers a relational view of
reality which can accommodate the modern findings
of physics, can do justice to Einstein and has
certain advantages in dealing with the perennial
problem of universality and concreteness, although all difficulties have not been resolved.
What is perhaps most promising, Panikkar indicates that what intellectually may seem to be a
vicious cycle is often a vital cycle.

Notes
Conclusion

[1] "Śreyān svadharma vigunah paradharmāytsvanusthitat/svadharmenidhanam śreya para dhrama bhayāvaha," Bhagavad Gita, III, 35.

[2] C. M. Rogers, "Dialogue Postponed," Asia Focus, 1970, pp. 211-19, quoted in Sharpe, Faith Meets Faith, p. 144.

[3] Leonard Swidler, "Editorial-Ground Rules for Inter-Religious Dialogue," Journal of Ecumenical Studies, vol. 15 (Summer 1978) no. 3, p. 413.

[4] See Bibliography under "On Panikkar."

[5] Panikkar, Trinity and the World Religions, p. 52.

[6] Balwant A. M. Parradkar, "Christian Encounter of Men of Other Faith," Religion and Society, vol. xiv, no. 2, June 1969.

Selected Bibliography

Works of Raimundo Panikkar

Books

Panikkar, Raimundo. La India: Gente, Cultura, Creencias. Madrid: Railph, 1960. Lettresur l'Inde, Tourani Casterman, 1963. L'India, Bercia: Morcelliana, 1964.

_____. Patriotismo y Cristiandad. Madrid: Railph, 1961.

_____. Humanism y Cruz. Madrid: Railph, 1963.

_____. L'incontro delle religioni del mondo contemporaneo. Morfosociologia dell'ecumenismo. Roma: Edizionali Sociali, 1963.

_____. Die vielen Götter und der eine Herr. Beitrage zum ökumenischen Gespräch de Weltreligionen. Weilheim: O. W. Barth, 1963. Los dioses Y el Senor. Buenos Aires: Columba, 1967.

_____. Religion and Religions. Religione e Religioni. Berscia: Morcelliana, 1965. Religión y religiones. Madrid: Gredos, 1965. Religionen und die Religion. Munchen: Max Hueber, 1965.

_____. The Unknown Christ of Hinduism. London: Darton, Longman and Todd, 1964. Reprint 1968. Christus der Unbekannte im Himduismus. Luzern and Stuttgart: Raber Verlag, 1965.El Cristo desconocido del hinduismo. Madrid: Morava and Bercelona: Fontanella, 1970. Le Christ et l'hinduisme. Une présence cachée. Paris: Les Editions du Centurion, 1972. Il Cristo sconosciuto dell'Induismo. Milano: Vita e Pensiero, 1975.

_____. Kultmysterium in Hinduismus und Christentum:Ein Betrag zur vergleichenden Religiontheologie. Freiburg and Munchen: Karl Alber, 1964. Le mystére du culte dans l'hindouisme et le Christianisme. Paris: Les Editions du Cerf, 1970.

135

_____. *Maya e Apocalisse. L'incontro dell'induismo e del Cristianesimo.* Roma: Abete, 1966. *Misterio y Revelación. Hinduismo y Cristianismo: encuentro de dos culturas.* Madrid: Morava, 1971.

_____. *Kerygma und Indien.* Zur heilgeschichtlichen *Problematic der Begenung mit Indien.* Hamburg: Reich Verlag, 1967.

_____. *Tecnica y Tiempo. La Tecnocrania.* Buenos Aires: Columba, 1967.

_____. *L'homme qui devient Dieu. La foi dimension constitutive de l'homme.* Paris: Aubier, 1970.

_____. *El silencio del Dios. Un mensaje del Buddha al mund actual. Contribución al estudio del ateismo religioso.* Madrid: Guadiana, 1970.

_____. *Worship and Secular Man. An essay on the liturgical nature of man, considering Secularization a major phenomenon of our time and Worship as an apparent fact of all times. A study towards an integral anthropology.* London: Darton Longman and Todd, and N.Y. Orbis Books, 1973.

_____. *The Trinity and the Religious Experience of Man. Icon, Person. Mystery.* London: Darton, Longman and Todd and N.Y. Orbis Books, 1973. Revised edition of *The Trinity and the World Religions. Icon, Person. Mystery.* Madras: The Christian literature and Society, 1970. Reprint London DIT and N. Orbis, 1975.

_____. Algunos aspectos de la espiritualidad hindu. For *La Espiritualidad Comarada*, Vol. III of *La Perfeccion Cristiana, Vida y Teoría.* Edited by Baldomero Jimenez Duque and Luis Sala Balust. Barcelona: Flors, 1969. Dp. 433-542. *Spiritualita indu. Lineamenti.* Bercia: Morcelliana, 1975.

_____. *The Vedic Experience. Mantramanjari: An Anthology of the Vedas for Modern Man and Contemporary Celebration.* Los Angeles and Berkeley, University of California Press, and.London: Darton, Longman and Todd, 1977.

_____. The Intra-Religious Dialogue. N.Y.
Paulist   Press, 1978.

_____. Myth, Faith and Hermeneutics. N.Y.
Paulist   Press, 1979.

_____. Salvation in Christ: Concreteness
and Universality the Supername. Published
privately from Santa Barbara, 1972.

Selected Articles

Panikkar, Raimundo. "Church and the World
Religions, "Religion and Society. Bangalore,
vol. 14, nr2, 1967.

_____. "Dialogue between Ian and Ray: Is
Jesus unique?" Theoria to Theory. Vol. I
(January, 1967), pp. 127-137.

_____. "Towards an Ecumenical Theandric
Spirituality," Journal of Ecumenical Studies.
Vol. V (Summer 1968).

_____. "Confrontation Between Hinduism and
Christ," New Blackfriers. Cambridge.
December 1968.

_____. "Christianity and the World Reli-
gions,"Christianity--Collective
Work--Patiala, Punjab University (1969), pp.
78-127.

_____. "The Myth of Incest as Symbol for
Redemption in Vedic India," Types of Redemp-
tion. Contribution to the Theme of the Study
Conference held at Jerusalem--14th to 19th
July, 1968. Jerusalem Hebrew University,
edited by R. J. Zwiwerblowsky and C. Jouco
Bleeker, London. E. J. Brill (1970), pp.
130-143.

_____. "Multi-Religious Experience," Angli-
can Theological Review, Vol. 73, no. 4, (Oct.
1971), pp.

_____. "Philosophy of Religion in the
Contemporary Encounter of Cultures," Contem-
porary Philosophies: A Survey. edited by
Raymond Klibansky. Firenze: La Nueva Italia
Editrice (1971), pp. 221-242.

_____. "Indology as Cross-Cultural Cata-
lyst,"Numen, Vol. XVIII, Fasc. 3 (1971), pp.
173-179.

_____. "The Theandric Vocation," Monastic
Studies. Nr. 8 (Spring, 1972), pp. 67-74.

_____. "The Meaning of Christ's Name in the
Universal Economy of Salvation," Evangalisa-
tion, Dialogue and Development. Documento
Missinalia. Rome (1972), pp. 195-218.

_____. "Christians and the So-called
Non-Christians," Cross Current. Vol. XXII,
no. 3, (Summer-Fall, 1972).

_____. "Philosophy and Revolution. The
Text, The Context and the Texture," Philosophy East and West, Vol. 3 (July, 1973), pp.
315-322.

_____. "Action and Contemplation as Catego-
ries of Religious Understanding," Main
Currents in Modern Thought. New Rochelle:
The Center for Investigative Education
(November-December, 1973), pp. 75-81.

_____. "Vac in the Śruti," God's Word Among
Men. (Papers in honour of Fr. J. Putz, S. J.
Edited by G. Gispert-Sauch, Vidyajyoti, New
Delhi, 1973, pp. 3-24.

_____. "The Category of Growth in Compara-
tive Religion: A Critical Self-Examination,"
The Harvard Theological Review, Vol. 66, No.
1 (Jan., 1973).

_____. "Towards a typology of Time and
Temporality in Ancient Indian Tradition,"
Journal of Ecumenical Studies. Vol. XVIV, Nr.
2 (April, 1974), pp. 161-164.

_____. "Have 'Religons' the Monopoly of
Religion?", Journal of Ecumenical Studies
(Editorial), Vol. XI, Nr. 3, (Summer, 1974),
pp. 515-517.

_____. "The Silence of the Word: Non-dua-
listic Polarities," Cross-Currents, Vol.
XXIV, Nrs. 2-3 (Summer-Fall, 1974), pp.
166-171.

_____. "Echology," Monchanin, Vol. VIII,
Nos. 3-5 (June-December, 1975).

_____. "Temps at Historio dans la Tradition
del'Ine," in Los Cultures oi les Temps,
UNESCO. Paris (Payat), 1975, pp. 73-101.

_____. "The Mutual Fecundation," forward to
TheEmerging Culture in India. edited by Th.
Paul, Alwaye, Kerala, Pontifical Institute of
Theology and Philosophy, 1975, pp. 9-11.

_____. "Singularity and Individuality. The
Double Principle of Individuation," Revue In-
ternationale de Philosophie. 'Methode et
Philosophie de l'histoire'.-Hommage a Raymond
Klibansky--Bruxalles, Nr. 111-112, Fasc. 1-2
(1975), pp. 141-166.

_____. "Seed-Thoughts in Cross-Cultural
Studies," ("Pensees dans la problematique
pluriculturelle") Monchanin, VIII, 3-4.
Cahier 50, (June-December, 1975), pp. 1-73.

_____. "Time and History in the tradition of
India, Kala and Kama," Cultures and Time.
Unesco Press, Paris, 1977.

_____. "Ecumenism in the Pluralistic Con-
text,"Jeevadhara, Vol. 7, no. 40,
July-August, 1977.

_____. "La philosophie de la religion devant
le pluralisme et la pluralité des religions"
in Pluralisme philosophique et pluralite des
religions. Proceedings of the Colloquium
organized by Institute di Filosofia, Roma;
edited by E. Castelli: Paris (Aubier), 1977,
pp. 193-201.

_____. "The Time of Death: the Death of
Time. An Indian Reflection," in La réflexion
sur la mort. Proceedings of le Symposion
International de Philosophie: Athens (Ecole
Libre de Philosophie 'Pleton'), 1977, pp.
102-121.

_____. "Man as a Ritual Being," Chicago
Studies, XVI, 1 (Spring, 1977), pp. 7-10.

_____. "The New Innocence" in Cross Currents, Vol. XXVII, Nr. 1 (Spring, 1977), pp. 7-28.

_____. "Creation and Nothingness. Creation: ex nihilo sed non in nihilum. Nothingness: ad quem sed non a quo," Theologische Zeitschrift. Volume in honour of Professor Fritz Buri: Basel, (Jahrgang 33, 1977), pp. 344-352.

_____. "Alternatives to Modern Cultures," The Whole Earth Papers. Voices from India. (Winter, 1978), Vol. 1, Nr. 5, pp. 14-15.

_____. "Man and His Spirituality," Forum for Correspondence and Contact. New York, Vol. 9, Nr. 2, (January, 1978), pp. 58-61.

_____. "Tolerancia, ideologia y mito," dialogos. Mexico (El Colegio de Mexico) (January/February, 1978), pp. 4-10.

On Panikkar

Cousin, E. "The Trinity and World Religions," Journal of Ecumenical Studies, vol. 7. nr. 3, Summer 1970.

_____. "Raimundo Panikkar and the Christian Systematic Theology of the Future," Cross Current, vol. 29, no. 2, Summer 1979.

Coward, H. A. "Panikkar's Approach to Inter-religions Dialogue," Cross Current, Summer 1979.

Devadas, N. "The Theandrism of Raimundo Panikkar and Trinitarian Parallels in Modern Hindu Thought," Forthcoming in Journal of Ecumenical Studies.

Griffiths, D. B. Christ in India. N.Y. Charles Scribner and Sons, 1966, Ch. 18.

Mulder, D. E. "Raymond Panikkar's Dialog Met Het Hindoeisme," Gereformeers Theologisch Tiydschrift, August 1969.

Nelson, B. "A New Science of Civilized Analysis: A Tribute to Panikkar, Cross Current, Summer, 1979.

Parradkar, B. A. M. "The Christian Encounter
with Men of Other Faith," Religion and
Society. Vol. 14, nr. 2, June, 1967.

Reetz, D. "Raymond Panikkar's Theology of
Religion," Religion and Society. Bangalore,
September, 1968.

Slater, Peter. "Hindu and Christian Symbols in
the Work of R. Panikkar," Cross Current,
Summer, 1979.

Catholics in Dialogue with Hinduism

Abhisiktananda, (Henri Le Saux). An Indian
Benedictine Ashram, Tiruchirapallii Shanti-
vanam; 1951 (with Fr. J. Monchanin) reprinted
as A Benedictine Ashram by Times Press,
Dougras, I. Ø. M., U. K., 1964.

_____. Ermites du Saccidanande, Touruni:
Casterman, 1956 (with Fr. Monchanin).

_____. Sagesso Lindouo Mystique Chrétienne:
du Vedànta \ la Trinité, Pairs: 1965.
Saccidananda: A Christian Approach to
Advaitic Experience. Delhi: 1974.

_____. Le rencontre de l'hindouisme et du
Christianisme. Paris: 1966. Hindu Christian
Meeting Point: within the Cave of the Heart,
Bombay: 1969.

Cuttat, J. A. La recontre des religions, Paris:
Auber, 1957. The Encounter of Religions with
an Essay on the Prayer of Jesus, New York:
Desclée: 1960.

_____. Spiritual Dialogue between East and
West, Delhi: 1964.

_____. Expérience Chrétienne et Spiritu-
alite. Paris: Orientale, Desclée, 1967.

Griffiths, Dom Bede. Christ in India, New York:
Charles Scribners and Sons, 1966.

_____. Vedànta and Christian Faith, Los
Angeles: The Dawn Horse Press, 1973.

Johanns, Pierre. A Synopsis of "To Christ
Through the Vedànta," Ranchi: Catholic Press,
Part I, Sankara, 1930; II, Ramanuja, 1931;
III, Vallabha, 1932; IV, Chaitanya (n.d.).

_____. Introduction to the Vedànta, Ranchi:
Catholic Press, 1938, 1943.

_____. La Pensée religieuse de l'Inde,
Paris: Tradition de Louis-Marcel Gaithier,
1952.

Klostermaier, Klaus. Hindu and Christian in
Verindaban, London: SCM Press, 1969. In the
Paradise of Krishna: Hindu and Christian
Seekers, Philadelphia: Westminister Press,
1971.

_____. Kristaridya: A Sketch of Indian
Christology. Bangalore: Christian Institute
of the Studies of Religion and Society, 1967.

Lacombe, Olivier. L'Absoln Selon le Vedanta, les
notions de Brahman et d'Atman dans the
systems de Cankara et Râmànoudja. Paris:
Paul Geuthmer, 1937, 1966.

_____. Chemins de l'Inde et philosophie
Chrétienne. Paris: Alsatia, 1956. Mattam,
Joseph. Land of the Trinity. A study of
Modern Christian Approaches to Hinduism.
Bangalore: TPI, 1975.

Monchanin, Jules. A Benedictine Ashram (with
Henri Le Saux). Revised edition, Times
Press: Douglas, 1964. (First published as
An Indian Benedictine Ashram.
Tiruchirapallii: Saccidananda Ashram, 1951.

_____. Ermites du Saccidànanda, Un essai
d'intégration chrétinne de la tradition
monastique de l'Inde (with Henri Le Saux),
2nd ed. Paris: Casterman, 1957.

_____. Ecrits Spirituels@ presentation
d'Edonard Duperray. Paris: Ed. du Centurion, 1957.

_____. Mystique de l'Inde, Mystere Chrétien.
Paris: Fayard, 1976.

Schreiner, Peter. "The Attitude of Catholic
    Theology Toward the Non-Christian Religions."
    Thesis submitted in partial fulfillment for
    Masters of Art Degree, Temple University,
    Oct., 1968.

Zaehner, Robert-Charles. The Comparison of
    Religions. Religion East and West. Boston:
    (First published as A Sunday Times, 1958);
    French tr.: Inde, Israel, Islam, Religions
    mystiques et révélations prophétiques.
    Paris: Desclée, 1965.

_____. The Convergent Spirit. London:
    Rontledge and Kegan Paul, 1963.

_____. The Catholic Church and the World
    Religions. London: Burns and Oates, 1964.

_____. Concordant Discord, the Interdepen-
    dence of Faiths, Oxford: Oxford University
    Press, 1970.

Articles

Abhisiktananda. "The Way of Dialogue," Inter-re-
    ligious Dialogue. Bangalore: CISRS, 1967.

_____. "Yoga et priero Chretienne," Revue
    Monchanin. Montreal: April, 1970.

_____. "Dialogue Postponed" (C. M. Rogers
    and Shivendra Prakash), Asia Focus 3, 1970.

_____. "Communication in the Spirit,"
    Religion and Society. Bangolore: Sept.,
    1970.

_____. "Yoga and Christian Prayer," Clergy
    Monthly. Nov., 1971.

_____. "Hindu Scriptures and Worship," (2
    parts) Word and Worship. Aug.-Sept., 1973.

_____. "The Upanishads and the Advaitic
    Experience," Clergy Monthly . December,
    1974.

Cuttat, J. A. "The Religious Encounter of East
    and West," Thought. (Fordham) XXXIII (1958).

_____. "Dialogue Chrétienne avec l'orient spiritual," Choisier 2, (1961).

_____. "The Meeting of Religions," in Relation among Religions Today, ed. by Moses Jung and others. Leiden: 1963.

_____. "Christian Experience and Oriented Spirituality," Concilium, 9, 1969.

Griffiths, Dom Bede. "The Advaita Experience and the Personal God in the Upanishads and Bhagavad Gita," Indian Theological Studies, Patristics and Indian Spirituality. Vol. XV, March, 1978.

Johanns, Pierre. "Christian Faith and Vedanta," Light of East. XIV, 1936.

_____. "The Quest of God in the Upanishads: Is Tattvamasi an Intuition," Light of East XV, 1937.

_____. "L'Avatar et la doctrine du Salut ou l'analogue de l'Incarnation dans l'hindouisme," Rythmes du Monde, no. 1, 1946.

Klostermaier, Klaus. "Hindu Christian Dialogue," Journal of Ecumenical Studies 5, 1968.

_____. "Hindu-Christian Dialogue: Its Religious and Cultural Implications," Studies in Religion, 1971.

Lacombe, Olivier. "La Mystique Naturell dans I'Inde," Revue Thomiste, 51, 1951.

_____. "La Pensée Catholique traditionnelle et l'hindouisme," Le Monde Non-Chrétien, 20, 1951. _____. "Elan spirituel de l'hindouisme," Bulletin du Cercle St Jean Baptiste, no. 24, Juin-Juillet, 1963. _____. "La Recontre du Christianisme avec l'hindouisme," Rythmes du Monde, XV, 1967. _____. "L'Absolu dans l'hindouisme," Religions, Thémes fondamentaux pour une connaissance dialogue, Rome, 1970.

Monchanin, Jules. "L'Eglise et la pensée Indienne," Bule des Missions 15 (1936).

144

_____. "L'Inde et la Contemplation," _Dieu_
Vivant, 1, 1945.

_____. "Le Temps Selon l'hindouisme et le
Christianisme," _Dieu_ _Vivant_, 4, 1949.

_____. "The Christian Approach to Hindus.
Some obstacles to conversion of Hindus to
Christianity," _India_ _Missionary_ _Bulletin_, 1,
1952-53.

_____. "The Quest of the Absolute," in _Indian_
Culture _and_ _the_ _Fullness_ _of_ _Christ_. Madras:
1957.

_____. "India and Contemplation," _Cross_
Currents, no. 4, 1958.

_____. "Problemes du yoga Chrétien," ed. by
S. Slauve, _Axes_ 8, 1969. Zaehner, R. C.
"Salvation in the Mahabharata," in _The_
Saviour _God_: Comparative Studies in the
Concept of Salvation. Ed. by Brandon,
Manchester, 1963.

_____. "Utopia and Beyond, Some Indian
Views," Eranos Jahrbuch, 39, 1963.

_____. "Learning from other Faiths: Hindu-
ism" Expos. _Times_, 83, 1972.

Christianity and Non-Christian Religions

Bouquet, A. C. _The_ _Christian_ _Faith_ _and_
Non-Christian _Religions_. London: Nisbet,
1958.

Devanandan, P. _The_ _Gospel_ _and_ _Renascent_ _Culture_.
London: S. C. M. Research pamphlet ᴕ8,
1959.

Dupuis, James. _Jesus_ _Christ_ _and_ _His_ _Spirit_.
Bangalore: Theological Publications in
India, 1977.

Farquhar, J. N. _The_ _Crown_ _of_ _Hinduism_, 1913.
Reprint, Delhi: Motilal Benarasidass, 1971.

Hillman, E. _The_ _Wider_ _Ecumenism_ _Anonymous_
Christianity _and_ _the_ _Church_. London: Burns
Oates and Harder ā Harder, 1968.

Kraemer, H. The Christian Message in Non-Christian World. Harper Bros., 1938.

Neill, Stephen. Christian Faith and Other Faiths. The Christian Dialogue with other Religions. Oxford: Oxford University Press, 1970.

Sharpe, E. Faith Meets Faith. London: S. C. M., 1977.

Steward, W. India's Religious Frontier: Christian Presenc Amid Modern Hinduism. London: S. C. M., 1964.

Vempeny, Ishananda. Inspiration in the Non-Biblical Scriptures. Bangalore: Theological Publications of India, 1973.

Hinduism

Scriptures

Bhakti-Vedanta, A. C. Swami. The Bhagavad Gita, As It Is. N. Y.: McMillan, 1968.

_____. Lord Caitanya in Five Features. Chapter 7, Adi-Lilā, of Krsna Kavirāja Gosvāmi's Sri-Caitanya-Caritāmrta. California: ISKCON Books, 1973.

Chidbhavananda, Swami. The Bhagavad Gita. S. India: Tapovanan Publishing House, 1967.

Deutsch, Eliot, trans. The Bhagavad Gita. N. Y.: Holt Rinehart and Winston, 1968.

Dutta, M. M. A Prose Translation of the Mahabharata. 18 vols., Calculta: H. C. Dass., 1895-1905. Edgerton, F. The Bhagavad Gita. 2 vols., Harvard: 1952.

Griffith, R. T. H. Hymns of the Rig Veda. 2 vols., Banaras: E. J. Lazarus, 1920-1936.

Hill, W. D. P. The Holy Lake of the Acts of Rama. N. Y.: Oxford University Press, 1952.

Hume, R. E., trans. The Thirteen Principal Upanishads. N. Y.: Oxford University Press, 1962.

Matthews, G., trans. Siva-Nāna-Bodham. Oxford: 1948.

Muller, Max. The Sacred Books of the East. Oxford:Clarendon Press, 1879-1910. Paperback by Dover Press in U. S. A. and Motilal Banarasidass, India.

Nallaswami Pillai, J. M., trans. Sīvajñāna Siddhiyar of Arunandi Sīvacārya. Madras: 1913.

Nikhilananda, Swami. The Gospel of Ramakrishna. New York: Ramakrishna vivekananda Center, 1942.

Prabhavananda, Swami and Frederick Manchester. The Upanishads. Hollywood, Calif.: The Vedanta Press, 1947.

Radhakrishnan, Sarvapalli, ed. and trans. The Principal Upanishads. London: George Allen and Unwin, 1953.

Radhakrishnan, S. and Charles A. Moore. A Source Book of Indian Philosophy. Princeton: Princeton University Press, 1967.

Sanyal, J. M., trans. The Srimad Bhagavatam. 5 vols., Calcutta: Oriental Publishing Co., 1952-1954.

Sastri, H. P., trans. Narada Sutras. London: S. Sadan, 1963.

Thomson, E. J. Bengali Religious Lyrics, Sakta. Calcutta: 1923.

Wilson, H. H., trans. The Visnu Purāna. Calcutta: Punthi Pustak, 1961.

Zaehner, R. C., trans. Hindu Scriptures. N. Y.: Dulton, paperback ed., 1966.

_____. Bhagavad Gita. London: Clarendon Press, 1969.

General Readings on Vaisnavism, Śaivism and Śāktaism

Avallon, A. Śakti and Shākta. Madras: 1929.

Bhaktivedanta, A. C., Swami. The Teachings of
Lord Chaitanya. N. Y.: International Soc. of
Krishna Consciousness, 1968.

Bhandarkar, R. G. Vaisnavism, Śaivism and Minor
Religious Systems. Straussburg: 1913.

Bharati, Agehananda. The Tantric Tradition.
Garden City, N. Y.: Doubleday Anchor, 1970.

Bhattachryya, Haridas, ed. The Cultural Heritage
of India. Vol. IV, The Religions. Calcutta:
Ramakrishna Institute of Culture, 1956.

Chatterjee, J. C. Kashmir Saivism. Srinagar:
1914.

De, S. K. Early History of Vishnava Faith and
Movement in Bengal. Calcutta: K. L.
Mukhopadhya,1942.

Dhavamony, M. Love of God According to Sàiva
Siddhanta. Oxford: 1971.

Gonda, J. Aspects of Early Visnuism. Utrecht,
1954.

_____. Visnuism and Śaivism. A comparison.
London: University of London. The Athlone
Press, 1970.

Mahadevan, T. M. P. The Idea of God in Śaiva
Śiddhànta. S. India: Annamalai University,
1955.

Rawson, P. S. Tantra. London: Arts Council,
1971.

General Readings on Hinduism

Chatterjee, S. The Fundamentals of Hinduism.
Calcutta: Das Gupta, 1950.

Hopkins, T. J. The Hindu Religions Tradition.
Encino, California: Dickenson Publishing Co.,
1971.

Johanns, P. La pensée religieuse de l'Inde.
Namur, Fac. University, Paris: J. Vrin and
Louvain Nauwelaerts, 1952.

Lacombe, O. Chemins de l'Inde et philosophie Chrétienne. Col. 'Sageese et Cultures.' Paris: Alsatia, 1956.

Mahadevan, T. M. P. Outlines of Hinduism. Bombay: Chetana, 1956.

Mehta, P. D. Early Indian Religious Thought. London: 1956.

Nikhilananda, Swami. Hinduism. London: Allen á Unwin, 1958.

Renou, L. Religions of Ancient India. London: 1953.

Sharma, D. S. A Primer of Hinduism. Madras: 1923.

Walker, B. Hindu World: An Encyclopaedic Survey of Hinduism. London: George Allen á Unwin. 2 vols., 1968.

Zaehner, R. C. Hinduism. N. Y.: Oxford University Press, 1962.

Buddhism

Jaytileki. Early Buddhist Theory of Knowledge. London: Allen á Unwin, 1963.

Murti, T. R. V. The Central Philosophy of Buddhism. London: Allen á Unwin, 1955.

Nàgàrjuna. Mùlamàdhymikakàrikà. Tr. K. Inada, Tokyo: The Hokusiedo Press, 1970.

Poussin. Way to Nirvana. Cambridge: Cambridge University Press, 1917.

Stchenbatsky, Theodore. Buddhist Logic. 2 vols. New York: Dover, 1962.

Catholic Doctrines

Bonaventure. The Works of Bonaventure. Seraphic doctor and saint. Tr. from Latin by José de Vinck, Paterson, N. J.: St. Anthony Guild Press, 1960-70.

Cousins, E., Tr. Bonaventure. N. Y.: Paulist
    Press, 1978.

Daniélou, Jean. A History of Early Christian
    Doctrine. Vol. 2. Philadelphia: Westminister
    Press, 1973.

Denzinger, H. J. D. (1819-1883). The Sources of
    Catholic Dogma; tr. by Roy J. Defferrari from
    30th ed. of Enchiridion Symolorum. St.
    Louis: Herder, 1957.

Dupis, James, S. J. Jesus Christ and His Spirit.
    Bangalore: TPI, 1977.

Kung, Hans. On Being a Christian. Garden City,
    N. Y.: Doubleday, 1974.

Lawson, John. A Theological and Historical
    Introduction to the Apostolic Fathers. New
    York: Mcmillan, 1961.

Louis, R. The Achievements of Karl Rahner. New
    York: Harder and Harder, 1967.

Neuner, J. The Teachings of Catholic Church as
    Contained in her Documents. Originally
    prepared by J. Neuner and Heinrich Roos, ed.
    K. Rahner, tr. by G. Stevens. Staten Island,
    N. Y.: Alba House, 1967.

Neuner, J. and J. Dupis (eds.). The Christian
    Truth. Dublin: Mercier Press, 1973.

Papali, C. B. "Excursus on Hinduism," Commentary
    on the Doctrines of Vatican II. Vol. 3. N.
    Y.: Harder and Herder, 1969.

Rahner, Karl. Christian at the Cross Road. N.Y.:
    Seabury Press, 1975.

_____. Foundation of Christian Faith. N. Y.:
    Seabury Press, 1978.

_____. Trinity. Tr. J. Donceel. N. Y.:
    Harder and Harder, 1970.

Roberts, A. and J. Donaldson, trs. and eds. The
    Ante-Nicene Fathers. Buffalo: The Christian
    Literature Publishing Co., 1885-97.

Schoonenberg, P. The Christ. N. Y.: Seebury
Press, 1971.

Wiles, M. The Christian Fathers. London:
Hodden ā Stonghton, 1966.

_____, ed. Documents in Early Christian
Thought. Cambridge and N. Y.: Cambridge
University Press, 1976.

Hindus on Christ and Christianity

Akhilananda, Swami. Hindu View of Christ. N. Y.:
Philosophical Library, 1949.

Devadas, Nalini. Sri Ramakrishna. Bangalore:
1965.

Gandhi, M. K. The Message of Jesus Christ. Ed.
and published by Anand T. Hingorani. 1st ed.
Bombay: Bharatiya vidyabhavan, 1940.

_____. Christian Missions. Ahmedavada: 1940.

_____. The Collected Works. Delhi: The
Publication division of the Ministry of
Broadcasting, 1958.

_____. All Men are Brothers. Life and
Thoughts of Mahatma Gandhi as told in his own
words. Compiled and edited, Krishna Kripa-
lani, intro., S. P. Radhakrishnan.
Ahmedavad: Navajivan Publishing House, 1960.

_____. All Religions are True. Ed. and
Published by Anand T. Hingorani. Bombay:
Bharatiya vidya Bhavan, 1962.

Harijan. Vol. 1-19. A Journal of Applied
Gandhism. Published from Ahmedavada. Reprint
by Garland Publishing Inc., N. Y. and London,
1973.

Gambhirananda, Swami. Ramakrishna and His Unique
Message. London: Vedanta Centre, 1970.

McKain, ed. Christianity: Some Non-Christian
Appraisals. N. Y.: McGraw Hill, 1964.

Muller, Max. Ramakrishna: His Life and Sayings.
New York: 1930.

Neill, Stephen. The Study of Christian Church in India and Pakistan. Grand Rapids: Eordmans, 1970.

Nikhilananda, Swami. Gospel of Ramavrishna. op cit.

Parekkh, M. C. Brahmarshi Kesab Chandra Sen. Rajkot: Oriental Christ House, 1926.

Parrindan, G. Avatar and Incarnation. Princeton: Princeton University Press, Bollinger Series, 1969.

Prabhavananda, Swami. The Sermon on the Mount According to Vedanta. New York: Mentor, 1972.

Radhakrishnan, S. P. Eastern Religion and Western Thought. Oxford, Clarendon Press, 1940.

_____. "My Search for Truth," Religion in Transition. Ed. Vergalius Ferm, London: 1937.

Roy, Rammohan. The English Works of Raja Rammohan Roy. Allahavad: Panini Office, Bahadurganj, 1906. A reprint; New York: AMS Press, 1978.

_____. The English Work of Raja Rammohan Roy. Ed. Kalidas Nag and Debajyoti Burma. Calcutta: Sadharan Brahmo Samaj, 1945-47.

Romain Rolland. Prophets of New India. New York: 1930.

Schwitzer, A. A Psychiatric Study of Jesus. Boston: Beacon Press, 1948.

Sharma, D. S. The Renaissant Hinduism. Bombay: Bharatiya Vidya Bhavan, 1966.

Thomas, M. M. The Acknowledged Christ of Indian Renaissance. London: SCM, 1969.

Vivekananda, Swami. The Complete Works. Almora: Advaita Ashrama, 5th ed., 1931. A new 7 vol. ed. is published from Calcutta Advaita Ashrama, 1962, 14th ed., 1972.

Zimmer, H. Philosophies of India. Princeton:
Princeton University Press, Bollinger Series,
1951.

Vedânta

Alson, A. J. That Thou Art. Shanti Sadan, 29
Chapston Villas. London: W. II, 1967.

Amalananda. Kalpataru, Laksm'nrsimha, Son of
Konda Bhatta, Ābhogah: Kalpatarn Vyākhya, an
exhaustive commentary on Kalpataru. Ed.
with intro. and notes by Polegam Sri Rāma
Sastri and S. Subrahmnya Sastri. Madras:
Govt. Oriental Manuscripts Library, 1955.

Carman, J. B. The Theology of Ramanuja: An
Essay in Interreligious Understanding. New
Haven: Yale University Press, 1974.

Chaudhury, B. Upanisad, (Samkara Ramanuja
darsan). Sri Deviprasad Chattopadhya.
Calcutta, 20 (1378 Bengli Year) 1975.

Chaudhury, Roma. Ten Schools of the Vedanta,
Part 1 and 2. Calcutta: Rabindra Bharati
University, 1975.

Chidbhavavananda, Swami. Ramakrishna Lives
Vedanta. Tirupparaittami (India): Tapovanam
Publishing House, 1962.

Das, R. Introduction to Shankara. Calcutta:
Firma K. L. Mukhopadhya, 1968.

Das, S. K. A Study of Vedanta. 2nd ed. Calcutta: University of Calcutta, 1937.

Das, Gupta, S. N. A History of Indian Philosophy. Five volumes, Cambridge: Cambridge
University Press, 1940.

Deussen, Paul. The Systems of Vedanta. New York:
Dover, 1973.

Devaraja, N. K. A Source Book of Sarnkara.
Varanasi: Banaras Hindu University, (Delhi,
Motilal Benarasidass), 1971.

Dharmaraaja Diksita. Vedāntaparibhāsa. Translated and noted by Swami Madhavananda, with foreword by S. N. Das Gupta, 2nd ed., Howrah, Belur Math, Ramakrishna Mission Sarada Pitha, 1953.

Gambhirananda, Swami, Tr. Eight Upanisads with Sanikara's commentary. 2 vols. Calcutta, Advaita Ashrama, 2nd ed., 1966.

Ghate, V. S. The Vedanta: A Study of the Brahmasutras with the Bhasyas of Samkara, Ramanuja, Nimbarka, Madhva, and Vallabha. Poona: Bhandarkar Oriental Research Institute, 1960.

Gonda, J. Notes on Brahman. Utrecht: 1950.

Griffiths, D. B. Vedanta and Christian Faith. Los Angeles: The Dawn Horse Press, 1973.

Neevel, W. G. Jr. Yāmuna's Vedānta and Pāñcarcātra: Integrating the Classical and the Popular. Harvard: Harvard Dissertation in Religion 10, Scholar's Press, 1977.

Padmapāda. The Pañcapādikā of Padmapāda, ed. Rāma Sastri Bhagavatacharya. Beneras: E. J. Lazarus, 1891.

_____. Padmapāda. Tr. in English by Rājasevāsakta D. Venkataramiah. Boroda: Oriental Institute, 1948.

Prakasananda, Swami. The Vedanta Siddhantamuktavali of Prakasananda with English tr. and notes by Arthur Venis. 2nd ed., Beneras: Jagrnath Prasad, 1922.

Radhakrishnan, S. P. Indian Philosophy. 2 volumes. London: George Allen á Unwin, first published 1923, reprint, 1948.

_____. The Brahma Sutra: The Philosophy of Spiritual Life. London: Allen á Unwin, 1960.

Raghavachar, S. S. Sri Ramanuja On the Upanishads. Madras: Vidya Press, 1972.

154

Ramanuja. Vedārthasamgraha. Introduction,
critical ed., and annoted trans., A. B. van
Buitenen, Poona: Deccan College Postgraduate
and Research Institute, 1956.

_____. Sribhāsya of Ramanuja. Ed. and tans.,
R. D. Karmakara. Poona: University of Poona
Sanskrit and Prakrit Series, Vol. 1, three
parts, 1959-64.

_____. Brahmasutra-Sribhāsya with Srutapra-
kāsika of Sudarsanasūri. ed. U. T. Vira-
rāghavācārya. 2 vols. New Delhi: Govt. of
India, 1967.

_____. Srimadvagavadgita, ed. Abhinava Desika
(uttamur) T. virarāghavācharya. Madras:
Ubhaya Vedanta Granthamala, 1972.

Rangarāmānuja. Chāndogyopanisad, Sampadakah
(ed.) Uttamurti, virarādhavacārya. Tinupati,
Timmali: Tirupata Sri Venkate
Saradevasthānamundrāsāliya, 1952.

_____. Kenopanisadbhāsyam. Critically ed.,
with intro. and English trans. and notes, K.
C. Varadachari and D. T. Tatachārya. Tiru-
pati: Sri Venkatesvra Oriental Institute,
1945.

Sadananda Yogindra. Vedanta Sara. Ed. and
trans., Nikhilananda. Calcutta: Advaita
Ashrama, 1968.

Samkara. The Bhagavad-Gita. English tr; A.
Mahadevasāstri, 2nd ed., Mysore: N. P.,
1901.

_____. Anandalahari. Tr. and commentary, A.
Avalon. Calcutta: Printed by S. C. Chowd-
hury, 1917.

_____. Viveka-cudamani. English trans., M.
N. Chatterjee. 2nd ed. Madras: Theosophical Publishing House, 1974.

_____. Upadeshasahasri. Tr. and explanatory
notes, Swami Jagadananda. 2nd ed. Mylapore:
Ramakrishna Math, 1949.

155

_____. Brhadãranyaka Upanisad. Tr., Swami
Mãdhavãnanda. Mayavati Almora: Advaita
Ashrama, 1950.

_____. Bhagavad Gita with the Commentary of
Sri Sankarãcãrya. Ed., Dinakar Vishnu
Gokhale, Poona, Oriental Book Agency, 1950.

_____. Ten Principal Upanisads with Sãnka-
rabhãsya. work, of Sankarãcãrya, vol. 1,
Delhi: Motilal Banarsidass, 1964.

_____. Aitareyopanisad. Svanuvãda Samka-
rabhãsya Sahita. Gorakhpur: Gita Press,
1965.

_____. Mundakopanisad. Text, English and
Bengali trans., Sankarabhãsya and critical
notes, K. Ray. Calcutta: K. Ray, 1965.

_____. Daksinãmurtistrotra of Sri Sankara-
charya and Dakshinamurti Upanisad with Sri
Sureswarãchãrya's Mãnasollasa and
Pranavavãrtika. Text and English trans.,
Alladi Mahadeva Sastry; with the introductory
essay "The Vedanta doctrine of
Sankaracharya." 3rd ed. Madras: Samanta
Books, 1978.

Sharma, B. N. K. The Brahmasutras and Their
Principal Commentaries. (A critical exposi-
tion.) Vol. II. Bombay: Bharatiya Vidya
Bhavan, 1974.

Singh, Satyavrata. Vedanta Desika: His Life,
Works and Philosophy. Varanasi: Chowkhamba
Sanskrit Series Studies, Vol. 5, 1958.

Sivananda, Swami. Bliss Divine. The Yoga
Vedanta Forest Academy, 1964.

Sudarśana Bhatta. Bhagavad Vãdarayana pranitã
Brahmasutra bhãsya, Sãrirakamimãmsã bhãsya.
Sri Bhagavad Rãmãnujaviracitam Sri bhãsysam,
Sri Sudarsãnamun viracita
sutrasindhu--Sutraprakasikasya Vyãkhya--
samundrasahita, . . ., Madras:
Uvayavedãntagrathamala, 1967.

Suresvaracãrya. Naishkarmasiddhi. Ed. and
annoted, Pandit Rãma Sastri, Manavalli.
Beneras: B. B. Dass, 1904.

_____. The Sambandha-Vartika. Ed. and
English trans., intro., notes, and extracts
from three unpublished commentaries, T. M. P.
Mahadevan, Madras: University of Madras,
1958.

Vàcaspatimisra (disciple of Martan datilaka
Swami). The Bhàmati of Vàcaspati on Sankara's
Brahma Sturabhàsva (catussutri). Ed., and
English trans., S. S. Suryanarayana Sastri
and C. Kunhan Raja, foreward, S. Radhakrishnan. Madras: Theosophical Publishing House,
1933.

van Buitenen, J. A. B. Ramanuja on the Bhagavad-
gita, a condensed rendering of his Gitabhasya
with copious notes and introductions,
'S--Gravenhage, H. L. Smits, 1953.

_____. A Source Book of Advaita Vedanta.
Hawaii: University Press of Hawaii, 1971.

Yamunacàrya. Ramanuja's Teachings in His Own
Word. Bombay: Bharatiya Vidya Bhavan, 1963.